NOTES FROM THE UPSIDE DOWN

INSIDE THE WORLD OF STRANGER THINGS

THE UNOFFICIAL GUIDE TO THE HIT TV SERIES

EBURY
PRESS

NOTES FROM THE UPSIDE DOWN

INSIDE THE WORLD OF STRANGER THINGS

THE UNOFFICIAL GUIDE TO THE HIT TV SERIES

GUY ADAMS

3 5 7 9 10 8 6 4

Ebury Press, an imprint of Ebury Publishing
20 Vauxhall Bridge Road
London SW1V 2SA

Ebury Press is part of the Penguin Random House group of companies
whose addresses can be found at global.penguinrandomhouse.com

Penguin
Random House
UK

First published by Ebury Press in 2017

www.penguin.co.uk

A CIP catalogue record for this book is available from the British Library
ISBN 9781785036439
Printed and bound in Great Britain by Clays Ltd, St Ives plc

CONTENTS

INTRODUCTION

Ah ... remember the eighties? Things were simpler back then: we had a divisive, ruthless woman in Downing Street, a tanned showboating Republican in the White House and all we had to worry about were rumblings from Russia and violence in the Middle East. Happy days. I doubt we'll see their like again.

The world of television was certainly simpler. We had limited choices, and those we did have were more ephemeral. Yes, you might be lucky enough to video your favourite show (if you could afford the tape), but chances are, once you'd seen it, it was gone. But that was OK, because we had books, novelisations so we could relive the story (only with better special effects) and maybe even books *about* the show so we could find out what exactly it was that a producer did, and what else we'd seen that bloke on the left in, no that one, yes, the one holding the plastic ray gun while lumps of fibreglass from the planet Alpharis descend on him.

Of course, now, we have streaming, we have downloads, we have TV that never goes away. As for books, who needs them? That's what the Internet's for.

Oh. Hello. Welcome to *Notes from the Upside Down: Inside the World of Stranger Things*. I'm a book. Sorry.

Maybe I'm just another eighties reference. A nostalgic wink.

So what's the point of me?

Well, on the one hand, I can but hope that some of the people picking me up aren't so immersed in the show that I can't tell them a few things they didn't know. That would be nice. I have lots of facts; enjoy them, sprinkle them into dinner conversation until all your guests leave (at which point fire up Netflix and watch something, who needs friends?).

For the rest of you, the ones who know *everything*, I hope you'll find plenty of interest here too. I particularly hope you find things – movies, TV shows, books – linked to the show that you didn't know so much about and maybe haven't seen or read. I would like that very much. If this book makes just one person watch Gary Sherman's 1981 movie *Dead and Buried*, I shall consider my time well spent.[1]

Most of all, I hope this book is simply this: a fun conversation – albeit a rather one-sided one, sorry, feel free to shout back – between fans of the show. When you love something it's nice to go on about it a bit, isn't it? This is me. Going on.

Here's how it works: as well as couple of general sections looking at the creation of the show and the cast involved, we'll look at each episode and – as well as boring you with my opinion[2] – I'll talk about references the episode contains, songs featured, I'll even highlight the odd member of guest cast for special consideration. Because Andrew Benator deserves his name in a book, don't you think?[3] I'll also be discussing the major influences on the show, from Stephen King to Steven Spielberg, Drew Struzan to Richard Greenberg. I'll talk about secret government projects, and

---

1   I will discuss other films too, don't worry, it was just the first to spring to mind.

2   See? It's not dissimilar to the Internet after all.

3   Twice, Andrew, TWICE!

Dungeons and Dragons and … oh, you know, fun stuff.[4]

There's even a quiz. I KNOW.

So, to hell with the Internet; just for a minute, let's pretend it's the eighties again. Let's remember when there was nothing better than a dense, excitable sourcebook detailing worlds of the imagination.

Roll ten or more to turn the page and let's have fun.

STRANGE BIRTH

So, everyone likes *Stranger Things*, yes? You can't move for people wafting frozen egg-based foodstuffs around and bopping to the ominous synth pulsing of John Carpenter, certainly not in my house. So it must have been an easy show to get on our screens?

OF COURSE NOT.

This is TV, nothing is ever easy in TV.

Though, in fairness, despite the odd speed bump, *Stranger Things* had an easier ride than some. Before we delve deeper into minutiae and wallow in the murky, mad old business of dissecting the show as if it were a rubber-and-kapok-stuffed faux Will Byers, let's treat ourselves to a BMX bike-ride through the UFO-lit forest of its creation.

---

4   And there are footnotes, too! How nice is that? I like to think of it as the literary equivalent of the Upside Down. A place that's like the real world but a bit pokier and harder to travel to.

THE DUFFER BROTHERS

Ross and Matt Duffer are twins, fraternal or identical they don't know and they're in no rush to find out. They were born in 1984 and grew up in the middle of nowhere in Durham, North Carolina. As any fantasist knows, the middle of nowhere is an easy place to escape from; all you need is a good book or movie. A love of the likes of Spielberg, Stephen King and John Carpenter struck early on, as they wrote in an essay for *Entertainment Weekly*:

"We were pretty ordinary kids growing up in the suburbs of North Carolina, and when we watched these films and read these books, it made us feel like our rather normal lives had the potential for adventure. Maybe tomorrow we would find a treasure map in the attic, or maybe one of us would vanish into the television screen, or maybe there was a clown in that sewer grate down the street."

Speaking to Vulture.com, Ross would add: "Why we loved this stuff so much is because these movies and books were about very ordinary people we could relate to, that we understood … That was always our favourite type of story, and that's the stuff we fell in love with. The peak of those type of ordinary-meets-extraordinary stories was in the '80s."

So, yes, the Duffer Brothers were dreamers. They were basically Mike, Dustin, Lucas and Will.[5] More, I'm betting they were everyone that's reading this book.

Take the middle of nowhere, add a sizeable amount of

---

5   Although they played the card game Magic: The Gathering rather than Dungeons and Dragons.

escapist fantasy and it's only a matter of time before a kid starts making things up themselves. The Duffer Brothers began making movies by fourth grade.[6]

In an interview with North Carolina's *The News & Observer*, they claimed that their first directorial obsession was with the work of Tim Burton.[7] They thought his movies, especially when you're young, were incredibly visual and distinct. They were able to recognise the job of director and identify with Tim's movies.

Their first homemade movie was based on Magic: The Gathering and was effectively just the two of them beating one another with plastic swords.[8] We all have to start somewhere. They had no editing equipment and the soundtrack consisted of Danny Elfman music played live through a tape recorder.[9]

For all they consider their first attempts unwatchable, a habit was formed and every summer they would make a new movie. It's no great surprise that they ended up studying film in California at Chapman University. While studying, they continued making short movies, including *We All Fall Down* about the bubonic plague in 1666, which won Best Short at the Deep Ellum Film Festival in 2005.

---

6   Year five in the UK, meaning they were around nine or ten. The Duffer Brothers aren't entirely sure.

7   Two of Burton's early films, of course, *Beetlejuice* (1988) and *Edward Scissorhands* (1990), starred Winona Ryder.

8   Some might argue Michael Bay's career has managed to do little more than this, with oodles more money, for years.

9   Noted soundtrack composer who has worked extensively with Tim Burton.

For their senior thesis they adapted the short story *Eater* by Peter Crowther,[10] which can be viewed in its entirety online[11] and which secured them representation by the Paradigm Talent Agency. Things seemed to be on the up and they sold a script for their first full-length feature, *Hidden*, to Warner Bros with both of them attached as directors.

Hidden tells the story of a family in a fallout shelter, hiding from the after effects of a viral outbreak. Alexander Skarsgård and Andrea Riseborough were cast and it seemed the Duffer Brothers' big break was on the cards. Sadly, the studio delayed the release of the movie for three years (even then it only crept out on VOD). While they were waiting, they pitched ideas for the studio's planned adaptation of the Stephen King novel *It* but were turned down.

Luckily, all was not lost; noted director M. Night Shyamalan had read, and liked, the script for *Hidden* and offered the Duffer Brothers a writer/producer job on the TV show he was developing, *Wayward Pines*. They ended up writing four episodes of the show's first season and, perhaps more importantly, learned a great deal about the process of making television.

Talking to *Rolling Stone* magazine, Ross said, "That became our training ground, and M. Night Shyamalan became a great mentor to us. By the time we came out of that show, we were like, 'OK, we know how to put together a show.' And that's when we wrote *Stranger Things*."

---

10   A story that has been adapted for the screen a couple of times, firstly for UK series *Urban Gothic* in 2001, then, again in NBC's *Fear Itself* anthology show, the latter directed by Stuart Gordon, the splendid director of such bravura Lovecraftian movies as *Re-Animator* (1985) and *From Beyond* (1986).

11   https://vimeo.com/11414039

DEVELOPING THE SHOW

The initial inspiration for their story was the 2013 movie *Prisoners*, starring Hugh Jackman. The movie told the story of a man desperately trying to find his abducted daughter.

"We thought, 'Wouldn't that movie have been even better in eight hours on HBO or Netflix?'" Matt told *Rolling Stone*. "So we started talking about a missing-person story."

In the same interview, Ross elaborated:

"It was great seeing those characters in that tone on the big screen, but we thought it needed more. It was taking that idea of a missing child and combining it with the more childlike sensibilities that we have. You know, can we put a monster in there that eats people? Because we are nerds and children at heart, we thought it was the best thing ever."

But they didn't want their monster to be magical; they wanted the show to be rooted in science rather than the supernatural. This led them to discuss stories of weird scientific experiments conducted during the Cold War, secret projects such as MKUltra.[12] They also had the realisation that setting the show in the eighties would not only fit the style of story they wanted to tell, but also allow them to pay homage to their childhood loves. They wrote a pilot script. Now all they had to do was sell it. Easy, right?

---

12   Discussed in detail later on in this book.

PITCHING

Well, it was easy to find a production company. Pitching the pilot script to networks, they met with rejection after rejection, fifteen to twenty in all. Networks didn't like the fact that the show centred on a group of kids and yet wasn't being pitched as a children's show. They had initially assumed Netflix – who had built a business model on producing shows from established names, not up-and-coming talent – wouldn't be interested, but when Dan Cohen and Shawn Levy at 21 Laps Entertainment came on board as producers, the Duffer Brothers were proved wrong. According to *The Hollywood Reporter*, Levy pitched to Netflix immediately and they bought it within twenty-four hours of the pitch.

PRODUCTION

Originally, the Duffer Brothers had wanted to set the show in a seaside town, thinking of Amity Island in *Jaws*. They settled on Montauk, New York due to the area's links with secret government experiments.[13] Ideas like that are fine on paper but when it comes to filming, practical issues get in the way. Talking to *The Hollywood Reporter*, Matt explained:

"It was really going to be impossible to shoot in or around Long Island in the wintertime. It was just going to be miserable and expensive. We're actually from North

---

13   Discussed in the same chapter as MKUltra ... I know, I'm such a tease, have patience.

Carolina, so when we wound up in Atlanta and I started scouting Atlanta we got excited about it, because it looked actually much more like our own childhoods."

Slowly the show we know is coming together, and with the casting, things fall into place even more. Carmen Cuba, casting director for a wide range of projects, from movies for Steven Soderbergh[14] to TV shows *Sense8* and HBO's *Looking*. It was Cuba who brought the suggestion of Winona Ryder to the table. The Duffers, Levy and Cohen immediately loved the idea, though not – as you might imagine – for reasons of nostalgia but simply because Ryder was a great actress who would bring a perfect quality to the show. A quality that ended up leaking into the script, as Matt told Bustle. com: "We knew she had a very specific energy and we thought we would lean into that, and that lead us to talking about Richard Dreyfuss's role in *Close Encounters* ... the idea of 'Winona Versus The World,' we loved that idea." Having recently enjoyed filming TV miniseries *Show Me a Hero*, Ryder read the script and signed up. She also brought a more unconventional idea to the role of Joyce Byers: her haircut. The actress wanted her to look like Meryl Streep in the movie *Silkwood*.[15]

Above all – as it should be – the casting simply came down to finding the best possible actors. In the case of Ryder and Modine they brought big, recognisable names, but that was

---

14   Director Soderbergh's biggest hits are certainly the *Ocean's Eleven* trilogy but Cuba worked with him on the movies *The Informant!*, *Contagion*, *Magic Mike* and *Beyond the Candelabra*.

15   A biographical movie from 1983 about Karen Silkwood who died in suspicious circumstances while investigating the nuclear power plant where she worked.

never the main interest on the part of the production team. To use David Harbour as an example, an actor who had a whole string of supporting roles behind him, it was decided that he would be perfect for the lead role of Chief Hopper.

"We just had a feeling that it was his time," says Levy in the same Bustle.com interview. "He took it and he made this choice that was simplicity, and about strength, and a depth of pain that he would very rarely show. You'll notice his performance is incredibly controlled. There is a stillness to Hopper that is so strong and so compelling on screen."

Of course, the greatest challenge would be in finding child actors. Ross admitted the danger to Vulture.com:

"We knew that a bad child performance would kill the show because so much rests on these kids' shoulders. What you're looking for are kids that feel real and naturalistic. Of course, watching *Stand By Me* is, to me, the pinnacle of child performances in movies or shows.[16] It doesn't get much better than that, and those kids, you feel like you know them instantly and they feel real. So many kids nowadays, it's almost like they go through this Disney training where they're taught to be cute and play it up for the camera, and they're trying to get laughs. What we were looking for were kids that, you just felt like you knew them."

Given *Stand By Me* was a touchstone for the Duffer Brothers, it's perhaps not surprising that they used scenes from the movie as audition scripts.

Carmen Cuba, in an interview with Backstage.com, points

---

16 Rob Reiner's 1986 adaptation of Stephen King's novella *The Body*. And a movie that gets mentioned SO many times in this book!

out a very important detail in that you're not casting kids, you're casting actors: "We needed every single actor to have a subtlety and an inner life that didn't necessarily need words to define them, and we held the kids and teens to the same standard. We didn't discuss it at the time, but it's clear that we weren't thinking of them as kid or teen actors … the Duffer Brothers were really expecting them to be able to deliver a very rich human experience despite what age body they were in."

Given the potential difficulties involved, the search was on from the moment the series was green lit. They ended up seeing over a thousand kids for the various roles. As there was still only the pilot episode written at this stage, the Duffer Brothers were able to tailor the characters to the actors they eventually found, willing to shift their initial ideas as new, better, possibilities became evident. A perfect example being the character of Steve, who became a lot softer, more rounded, thanks to the input of actor Joe Keery. Matt, talking to the *Daily Beast*, said:

"And this is what's so fun about television, even though we think of this as a big movie: movies aren't eight hours long. You're able to change things up a little bit. Steve initially was a stereotypical douchebag. He was a trope. And then a couple things happened and we found Joe Keery, this actor who didn't really fit our vision for Steve. But we just fell in love with this guy and wanted him in the show and kind of tailored the show for him. They thought Joe was charming and likable, even when he was being a douchebag in character, so they decided they would give him an arc."

Shooting began on a schedule of eleven days per episode,

slightly over average for a TV show. There was an added advantage that, with Netflix's release model – the entire series being available at once – episodes could be put to one side during the editing process and returned to later, allowing them to work on all eight as a whole, tweaking them once everything was in the can.

POST-PRODUCTION

Thinking in terms of the movies they had loved so much when they were young, the Duffer Brothers wanted to avoid using digital effects, but sadly that was impractical as Ross told the *Daily Beast*:

"… What we realized – and it really made us admire those guys who did *The Thing* and *Alien* and whatever – is that doing practical is really hard. It takes a lot of time and preparation. We were turning out scripts as quickly as we could, but they don't have six months to prep this stuff … It takes a lot of trial and error, so that was a lesson learned. At one point we tried to have the monster break through a wall practically and it just … It looked ridiculous.

"If anyone saw the test footage, they would be rolling on the floor laughing. So it was just us going, 'OK. Some of this we're gonna have to just do with visual effects.' But I think it's something that, for example, J.J. Abrams does a pretty brilliant job of. Like in the new *Star Wars*, he used a mix of both practical and visual effects and it's as seamless as possible. So for something like the lab, most of the vines and all that stuff throbbing and coming out of the hole, that's all production design. We built all that. But then where we needed to do stuff that we didn't have the time to figure out how to do practically, that becomes visual effects. It was a bit of 50-50 in the end.

For a lot of viewers a very important part of the post-production process, and a huge part of the overall atmosphere of the show, came with the soundtrack, composed by Michael Stein and Kyle Dixon.

As part of the initial pitch, the Duffer Brothers had spliced together a 'sizzle reel' of clips from the movies they loved partnered up with cues from director and composer John Carpenter. They knew they wanted an electronic score, something that could evoke that old sound, and they found it in the form of Austin band Survive, who had recently contributed to the soundtrack of Adam Wingard's movie *The Guest* (2014).[17] They contacted the band and Dixon and Stein came on board very early, even before actors were cast.

The duo composed a set of demos, to give an idea of the range they could bring to it – not just the horror moments but the quieter, emotional cues that would be needed – and the Duffer Brothers played the music while they were casting, just to keep in touch with the tone of what they were aiming for.

Both Stein and Dixon were also influenced by movies, quoting soundtrack artists such as Carpenter, Tangerine Dream, Giorgio Moroder and Goblin when interviewed in

---

17   For a modern spin on an eighties slasher – and therefore slightly outside the brief of this book but to hell with it – I heartily recommend Wingard's masterful 2011 movie *You're Next*.

Rolling Stone magazine. That said, they were quick to point out that they actually pushed for a more seventies tone musically, given that the eighties brought a colder, less rich electronic sound. "We're just drawn to seventies recording styles a little more," Dixon told the journalist, "I mean, eighties is great, and we love all that stuff too. But we try to make it sound a little warmer."

To say they succeeded is to state the obvious. Their music – along with tracks from other artists, which will be noted and discussed when we talk about individual episodes – is the backbone of the show, as Shawn Levy notes in an interview with Slashfilm.com: "… They were able to really cover a texture that not only gives a nod to that period, but I think also serves as an emotional storytelling device and a real core piece of the show, I think almost as a character. There were three storylines going on independent of one another for a while, and they bridge together in the sort of third act of the show. And I think one of the main things that connect them beyond family blood is this score that's kind of guiding them all together."

SCREEN

And then, on 15th July 2016, the show dropped. It's worth pointing out at this point that all TV shows involve the kind of effort we've merely skimmed the surface of above. Countless crews of people all pulling a thing into the world in the desperate hope it's going to land in front of an audience that like it. Many, many times, a show simply doesn't find the audience it needs.[18] Yes, those involved can hope – they can even make informed guesses – but you can never completely *know*. Would *Stranger Things* get the reception it deserved?

Just a bit.

You won't believe this, but some idiot even ended up writing a book about it.

---

18   We all have our list of shows that were not renewed that we loved, yes? I mean, honestly, what sane world does a show like *Hannibal* get cancelled? TELL ME THAT.

HOMEWORK

Peter Crowther, the author of the short story *Eater* that
the Duffer Brothers adapted for their final dissertation,
is a phenomenal author and anthologist who deserves
far more recognition than he gets (and he gets a fair bit:
his collection of stories, *Lonesome Roads*, won a British
Fantasy Award for Best Collection in 2000). His work has
the lyrical quality of Ray Bradbury and would certainly be
enjoyed by any fan of *Stranger Things* (as much as it clearly
was by the show's creators). So hunt down a copy of one
of his short story collections and get stuck in. It doesn't
matter which; once you've adored one I have every faith
you'll hunt down the rest anyway.

Pete is also a publisher: his company PS Publishing works
with authors such as Ramsey Campbell, Stephen King and
the late – and much missed – Ed Gorman.

NOTES

CHAPTER ONE

THE VANISHING WILL BYERS

anning down from the stars – a misleading visual
cue if ever there was one; the threat is not from
'out there' after all. We move into the corridors of
the Hawkins National Laboratory. It's owned by the US
Department of Energy, which makes the fact that the lights
are on the blink somewhat ironic. But to hell with the
reliable bulbs, no horror movie ever shot embraces terror
via fully functioning neon strips. Of *course* the lights must
flicker, we're about to meet something nasty. It's a Horror
Rule.[1] As is repeatedly stabbing the elevator button as if
that ever helped.[2] We pause for a while, as we must, that
all-important beat of silence where the character on screen
dares to hope all will be OK (even as the audience smile,
like the armchair psychos we are, knowing that it really,
really won't). Then, BOOM, the monstrous reaches down
from above and we cut to the whispering lawn hoses of
Middle America.

In less than two minutes of screen time we have some sense
of the show we're about to watch, but the real clincher is to
come once we're introduced to Mike, Dustin, Lucas and Will.
Four boys playing – for eleven hours straight, no less – a
Dungeons and Dragons campaign in Mike's basement den.
And with these four friends, and the promise of monsters it'll

---

1   Yes, yes, I know that intrusions from the Upside Down play havoc with the
     electrics but shush, it's done for atmospheric reasons above and beyond it
     being a plot point and you all know it.

2   One day someone will write a movie about petulant elevators who let
     people die by whatever's chasing them because (cue Muzak), "Like, you
     know, that stuff bruises you right in the diodes."

take more than the roll of a dice to beat, we've travelled back three decades to a type of horror fantasy unseen since – well, since J.J. Abrams riffed on the same notes in *Super 8*, if we're being really picky.

But don't mistake pernicketiness for criticism. Some have tried to write *Stranger Things* off as an over familiar bicycle ride through the dark woods of familiar tropes, but that's a disservice to what is a masterful homage, a homage that does what so few do: manages to stand on its own two feet. As Guillermo Del Toro pointed out on Twitter: "Stranger Things may be a lot of things: King, Spielberg, 80's, myself (Duffers pointed that out to me) but what it is, above all, is good!!"[3]

Yes. Good. Definitely. It's a show made by fans of fantasy and horror, particularly eighties fantasy and horror, to be watched by people that share the same passion. Look, those four main characters, resolutely geeky, bullied at school: I suspect most of us devoted Strangers can see a good chunk of our young selves in them, no?

And outside the wonderfully warm and familiar young cast we're introduced to Winona Ryder as 'Flaky Mom', David Harbour as 'Cop With A Past' and Charlie Heaton as 'Son Who Actually Has to Keep the Family Together' and if their characters are all rather broad strokes at first (how many times have we seen 'Cop With a Past' wake up amongst the

---

3   So said @RealGDT on 18th July 2016. Certainly Del Toro is no stranger to stories of the grotesque and fantastical as witnessed through the innocence of children. In fact, it's a constant theme through his early films. There is also little doubt that the Demogorgon, as a monster design, is something that wouldn't be out of place in a Del Toro movie (or a movie designed by H. R. Giger come to that, but we'll get to *Alien* (1978) at a later stage of the book).

detritus of booze and ashtray, only to pop a few pills just to keep him on an even keel?) that's OK because right now, broad strokes are what we need. We're building a world and a cast, there's time for detail and subtlety later.

It's Eleven who steals the show – some would say the whole series – with Millie Bobby Brown doing more with her eyes than an actor has any right to at such an age. All the young cast are good, don't get me wrong, but it's rare that you see someone so young possess such an assured, silent command of a screen. When she grows up, all the rest of the actors can go home.

There's a lovely detail to Nancy and Steve's relationship that proves that, while playing many familiar notes, *Stranger Things* will have fresh tunes for us. Past cinematic history has prepared us to hate Steve. He's the bastard boyfriend, he's the one who only wants one thing and, for all his early pretence, we just know he's only using Nancy until he gets it. Except he's not. He's far nicer, and when they do make out in Nancy's room, it's sweet and consensual rather than having that all-too-common undercurrent of 'Randy Boy Browbeats Pure Virginal Girl Until She Gives In'. That's a tired old trope and what a relief it is that we don't get it.

Oh my God! They killed Benny (sorry, couldn't resist).

And then there's Mathew Modine, the quiet, grey man who we just know harbours secrets that would turn our hair as white as his if only he were to whisper them in our ear.

It's a good job Netflix encourages us to binge-watch their shows because with such a solid, familiar and yet intriguing first episode, how could we not cue up episode two?

FAMILIAR THINGS

As tempting as it might be to point to every moment of tone and framing and call it a reference – and the Internet was certainly tempted, so tempted it ran with it wholesale [4] – I will resist. The opening of the show, with its flickering corridors, fleeing, soon-to-be-offcuts lab assistant and the final, inevitable death-from-above in the elevator may feel familiar, of course it does, but it's not so much tipping a wink to anything specific as simply telling us what sort of story were about to enjoy (as well, of course, as exciting us from the word go with a bit of running and death). It's the equivalent of a band pounding out a few familiar power chords to let you know what sort of tunes you can expect to be shaking your jolly body to in a few moments' time.

In truth – and as it should be – most of the references in *Stranger Things* are exactly these sorts of tonal touches; [5] they're familiar window dressing designed to make both those of us old enough to have ridden the eighties cultural wave the first time round and those who simply love wallowing in it second-hand feel a warm buzz of nostalgia.

---

4   "And, like, it's called *'Stranger Things'* which sounds like Stephen King's book *'Needful Things'*, doesn't it? Because they both have the word 'Things' in them!" This is not a reference, my dear, cherished, excitable friend. There are King references aplenty here, but at no point do Mike, Dustin and Lucas pop to a curio shop run by the Devil and sell their eternal souls through an act of mischief in order to afford that gorgeous Aurora Kit of Ghidrah the Three-Headed Monster. *Stranger Things* and *Needful Things* are similar in just the same way double-breasted gangster songfeast *Guys and Dolls* and women-in-prison pervathon *Barbed Wire Dolls* are similar.

5   And they're not all eighties tonal references either, the Duffer Brothers have also explicitly mentioned anime such as *Akira* and *Elfen Lied* and games such as *Silent Hill* and *The Last of Us*.

If I bothered to note every time the show hits a note
that reminds us of its forbears in a general sense – those
whispering lawn hoses less than two minutes in are such a
familiar touchstone of cinematic American domesticity, I'm
surprised they don't have their own IMDB entry – I would
have had to start writing this book back in the eighties
and you would soon be dead of boredom. So let's try to be
a bit choosy and stick to solid, specific references.[6]

THE ART OF THE TITLE

The Duffer Brothers were inspired by the work of Richard
Greenberg (see full article on 'The Look of The Show'
later on in this book). As well as a general homage to
Greenberg's work, the moment when each episode title
becomes transparent, revealing the following shot of the
show, is extremely similar to Greenberg's titles for David
Cronenberg's adaptation of the Stephen King novel, *The
Dead Zone*.

---

6   Which means I really shouldn't even mention that Mike's dad is watching
     Knight Rider on the TV a mere three and a half minutes in but I'm going to
     anyway, because if you can't take a minute to remember those halcyon days
     when we all thrilled to the adventures of David Hasselhoff and his talking
     Super Car, you might as well just give up on life. I personally preferred *Street
     Hawk*, which had an equally 'terribly injured but nursed back to life in order
     to fight the villain of the week' hero but this time plonked him on a Super
     Bike. Sadly nobody else did so it was axed after thirteen episodes. It did,
     however, have a theme by Tangerine Dream and we'll certainly talk about
     them later.

The Phoenix Rises

When Will Byers challenges Dustin to a bike race, the prize is a comic of his choosing. He plumps for issue 134 of the *Uncanny X-Men*.

The Marvel Comics series, after living on only in reprints for years, had been relaunched with phenomenal success under writer Chris Claremont (and, from issue 111, penciller and eventually co-plotter John Byrne). One of their most acclaimed stories was the Dark Phoenix saga.

Jean Grey, the sole female of the group when it launched back in 1963, had telekinetic (and eventually, telepathic) powers. During Claremont's run, Jean pushes herself beyond safe levels in order to save the people she loves. Rather than dying – as she seemed to do in true dramatic style – she became a far more formidable version of her old self and began calling herself Phoenix for a while. But those powers – as great powers always do allegedly – corrupted her and, in issue 134 no less, the lynchpin of the run, she becomes Dark Phoenix, a terrifying threat to all around her.

There are clear parallels to Eleven in Jean and only time – and the second series – will tell quite what form she'll find herself in after her own moment of heroic sacrifice.

Der DUM

The framing of the shot where Hopper begins typing up the police report regarding Will's disappearance is a direct homage to an identically framed shot in Steven Spielberg's *Jaws*.

Lord of the Rings … No! The Hobbit

Not an integral point perhaps, and we all know that Mirkwood, the name that the boys give the road Will travelled home on before his disappearance, is from *Lord of the Rings* … no, *The Hobbit*! But you may not know (and since a certain hairy New Zealander has dedicated whole lifetimes of celluloid to chronicling the stories of Tolkien, this is perhaps unlikely) 'Radagast', the code word to enter Will's den, is from the same book. It's the name of a wizard (played in Peter Jackson's movies by ex-Doctor Who Sylvester McCoy).

A Night at the Movies

Joyce offers Will tickets to see *Poltergeist*, a movie we'll discuss at greater length elsewhere. She also asks him …

Bob Gray

… If he's not still scared of clowns. Which might be a coincidence – because most sane people agree all clowns are evil – but, let's be honest, isn't. The monstrous creature in Stephen King's novel (which, again, we will discuss in more depth elsewhere) often appears as Pennywise, a flesh-eating clown.

The Ultimate in Alien Terror

There's a poster for *The Thing* (1982) on the wall. Yes, the boys love John Carpenter. Of course they do. So do the Duffer Brothers, but then, who doesn't?

STRANGER SOUNDS

No, not the lovely, squelchy synths of Michael Stein and Kyle Dixon but the songs heard during the show itself. The choice tunes selected by Nora Felder, music supervisor on the show, helped highlight some of our favourite moments.

In Benny's diner we hear two songs from psychedelic rock band Jefferson Airplane: 'She Has Funny Cars' and 'White Rabbit', both of which are taken from their 1967 album *Surrealistic Pillow*. We also hear (while Eleven indulges in some rather aggressive fan maintenance) 'Jenny May' from folk rockers Trader Horne.

When Hopper arrives at the police station, they indulge in banter while 1965's 'Can't Seem to Make You Mine' from the band The Seeds plays on the radio.

Meanwhile, Nancy has slightly more modern (well, no, not modern per se but you know what I mean) tastes. When Steve sneaks into her room, she's listening to 'Every Little Bit', a song by Jackie James and Ian Curnow. Curnow was the keyboard player for British New Wave group Talk Talk while Jackie James has worked mainly as a songwriter for other artists including Celine Dion, Jennifer Lopez, Kylie Minogue and (shudder) Steps, for whom she wrote the bestselling hit[7] 'Heartbeat'.

But you can't make out to 'Every Little Bit'. Well, you could have done perhaps until I told you that Jackie James later wrote songs for Steps. For making out you can't beat 'Africa' by Toto. It certainly works for Steve and Nancy.

---

7   The 's' is silent.

And while I promised I wasn't going to specifically mention the actual soundtrack, that final queue, when Eleven appears in the rain couldn't be more like Tangerine Dream if it tried.

REAL THINGS

On 6th November, 1983, Hawkins, Indiana loses one of its own and our fictional story begins.

In reality, the world had fears of its own. The monster that threatened to kill us all didn't come from the Upside Down, it came from the splitting of an atom.

The 6th is a Sunday, and Ronald Reagan is President of the United States. Four days earlier he had signed a bill to honour civil rights leader Martin Luther King Jr with a federal holiday to be held the third Monday of every January. While other cities and states have already established such holidays in King's honour, the first Martin Luther King Jr Day will be observed three years later in 1986 (though it isn't until the year 2000 that the holiday is celebrated country-wide). It's a welcome glimmer of positivity in a week that also saw Able Archer 83, a NATO exercise simulating a Western response to possible nuclear attack. The exercise is suspected as a ruse by the Soviets – a cover, perhaps for a genuine attack – who placed their own nuclear forces on alert. For the duration of the exercise, the Cold War becomes substantially hotter and the world hasn't been so close to nuclear war since the infamous Cuban Missile Crisis of 1962.

The weapons of war also rear their head in the UK as the first US cruise missiles arrive at RAF Greenham Common, south-east of Newbury in Berkshire. The announcement in June 1980 of the UK's intention to store cruise missiles at the site had seen the arrival of protesters outside the base and the establishment of the Greenham Common Women's Peace Camp, which was active for nineteen years, finally disbanding in 2000. Earlier that year around 70,000 protesters had formed a fourteen-mile human chain from Greenham to a nearby Ministry of Defence Atomic Weapons Establishment in Aldermaston. A month after the delivery of the US missiles, another demonstration took place with 50,000 women encircling the base. The fence to the base was breached several times and there were hundreds of arrests.

Outside of these constant concerns of war, November of that year also saw the infamous Brink's-Mat robbery take place. On the 26th, a gang of six raided a warehouse on the Heathrow International Trading Estate. They had expected a haul of £3.2 million in cash. They underestimated. They poured petrol over the security staff and threatened to set fire to them unless they revealed the combination numbers of the vault. Once opened, they found the vault contained three tonnes of gold bullion belonging to Johnson Matthew Bankers Ltd. They eventually stole £26 million in gold, diamonds and cash. Four of the robbers were never convicted and most of the gold was never found.

In popular culture, 6th November saw William Friedkin's movie *Deal of the Century*, a black comedy about arms dealers competing to sell weapons to a South American dictator (even here, the whiff of war) become number one at the US cinema box office.[8] It knocked Irvin Kershner's *Never Say Never Again*, a legally controversial movie that saw Sean Connery return to the role of James Bond outside the 'official' franchise, off the spot it had held for a month. Coincidentally, 1983 saw Mathew Modine's first film role, in John Sayles's *Baby It's You*.[9] The same year would see him – in substantially larger roles – appear in teen sex comedy *Private School*[10] and Robert Altman's *Streamers*, the entire cast of which won the Best Actor award at the Venice Film Festival.

In music, the number-one song that week was 'Islands in the Stream' from country music stars Kenny Rogers and Dolly Parton (with Lionel Ritchie encouraging us to party 'All Night Long' in the number-two slot).[11] In the UK, Billy

---

8   Most famous as the director of the ground-breaking *The Exorcist*.

9   Sayles, a talented writer and director, wrote the scripts for a handful of late seventies/early eighties horror movies that should be on every *Stranger Things* fan's Netflix queue: *Piranha* (1978), a joyfully nuts movie about how nothing spoils a summer holiday quite like a school of genetically-enhanced piranha fish (the first movie directed by Joe Dante, a director who also needs to be on your radar and will be discussed elsewhere); *Alligator* (1980), a movie about how nothing spoils a nice party like a genetically-enhanced alligator (spotting a theme?) and *The Howling* (1981), Dante's second movie and an absolute classic, offering a wonderfully knowing, modern spin on werewolves. If you really want a chuckle – and why wouldn't you? – you might also want to check out the delightfully trashy *Battle Beyond the Stars* (1980), a 'Magnificent Seven in space' movie with (cheap) special effects designed by a young James Cameron of *Avatar* fame. As an extra link to the show, on the strength of his work on *Piranha*, Sayles wrote a draft script for Steven Spielberg entitled *Night Skies*, a horror/sci-fi picture that Spielberg wanted Tobe Hooper to direct. The film never came to fruition but several elements from it would inform the scripts of both *E.T. The Extra-Terrestrial* and *Poltergeist*.

10   Three words to strike terror into the heart of movie consumers everywhere. Unless it's *Porky's* which is actually surprisingly fun.

11   Not a euphemism.

Joel was showing off about his 'Uptown Girl' while Paul McCartney and Michael Jackson's first of two duets 'Say, Say, Say' bubbled under at number two.

Two of the bestselling novels released that year were *Pet Sematary* and *Christine*, both by Stephen King. The former, about a pet graveyard that reanimates the things you bury there, he hesitated to submit, admitting in his introduction to the 1998 British edition, "I was horrified by what I had written …" As, of course, were we, deliciously so.

HONOURABLE STRANGERS

Bonus marks for guest cast members must go to Andrew Benator as 'Elevator Scientist'. He's the first actor we see and therefore receives the dubious honour of being the first person in *Stranger Things* to scream his head off in grisly circumstances. He's a familiar face to American viewers thanks to a string of commercials he shot for Citibank where he suffers various indignities in trying to deal with other banks.

I can't help but also mention Chris Sullivan as Benny, the nicest burger-flipper in Indiana. Sullivan has appeared in countless movies and TV shows where he manages not to die, including the current *This Is Us*, a comedy drama running on NBC in which he plays someone else who is utterly lovely.

HOMEWORK

Yes! A quiz! But not just any quiz, no, there will be no "What sort of waffle does Eleven like?" here. This is a quiz for champions![12]

1. When faced with the Demogorgon in Mike's D&D campaign, Will rolls the dice to throw a fireball. What score does he get? And what score did he need?

2. Dustin offers Nancy a leftover slice of pizza. What toppings does he specifically mention it has?

3. Joyce Byers has lost her car keys, where are they?

4. Bully Troy has nasty nicknames for Lucas, Mike and Dustin. What are they?

5. Phil Larson keeps having something stolen from his garden. What?

6. Hopper believes mornings are for two things. What are they?

7. What does Hopper consider to be the worst thing that has happened during the time he's served on the Hawkins police force?

8. Dustin wants to know whether Australians eat *what* for breakfast?

9. Who was Hopper's science teacher at school?

10. Which polymers occur naturally?

ADDITIONAL RESEARCH

The Howling (1981) Directed by Joe Dante

---

12 Or people happy to watch the episode again with a notebook, I'm not judging, there are no prizes beyond an insufferable sense of smugness and/ or self-righteousness if you disagree with any of my answers.

NOTES

THE DNA OF STRANGER THINGS: STEPHEN KING

"WATCHING STRANGER THINGS IS [LIKE] WATCHING STEVE KING'S GREATEST HITS. I MEAN THAT IN A GOOD WAY."

Stephen King – Twitter, 17th July 2016

"HE'S AMAZING, AND WHEN HE TWEETED ABOUT STRANGER THINGS, I WAS TRYING NOT TO CRY, BECAUSE THAT WAS RIGHT BEFORE THE PREMIERE AND IT REALLY FUCKED ME UP. IT WAS LIKE 20 MINUTES BEFORE WE WERE SUPPOSED TO GET IN THE CAR AND I'M LIKE, "I'M BARELY FUNCTIONAL RIGHT NOW."

Matt Duffer - Interviewed by Daniel Fienberg, *The Hollywood Reporter*, 1st Aug 2016

Stranger Things makes no bones about the dollops of Stephen King DNA buried in its genetic make-up. From its narrative to its title font it's a clear homage to the bestselling author.[13]

Born in Portland, Maine in 1947, his father left the family when King was only two years old. Claiming he was only popping to the store for a pack of cigarettes he simply never returned, leaving King's mother, Nellie Ruth, to bring both him and his older brother David up on her own.

King's childhood, unsurprisingly, was that of a dreamer.

---

13   When initially pitching the show to Netflix, they came up with a document that would show the look and atmosphere of the show, one of the images for which was King's novel *Firestarter* with the text swapped out for the show font and a solitary, abandoned bike added as a graphic.

The family was poor, his mother balancing caring for her sons with looking after her infirm parents and then, after they passed away, by working in the kitchens of a residential facility for the mentally challenged. Having found a collection of short stories by H.P. Lovecraft that had belonged to his father, King fell in love with horror.[14]

He started writing for fun while at school, and even earned money at it, selling stories based on popular movies to his fellow students. When his teachers discovered this they forced him to return the money.

Moving to the University of Maine (where he would meet his wife, Tabitha, also a novelist) he continued to write stories and a column for the student newspaper. He graduated with a B.A. in English, intending to work as a high school teacher but was unable to find an immediate post. Now married (and raising their first child, Naomi), they lived from King's wages working at an industrial laundry,[15] Tabitha's student loan and the occasional sale of a short story to magazines such as *Cavalier*. King finally gained a teaching post in the autumn of 1971 at the Hampden Academy in Maine, continuing to write in the evenings.

---

14   H. P. Lovecraft, a writer of weird horror tales, achieved most of his fame posthumously. He died in utter poverty at the age of forty-six but has gone on to become one of the most influential – and imitated – writers in horror.

15   An experience he would draw on for 'The Mangler' (first published in 1972), a short story about an industrial clothes press that becomes possessed by a demon, taking on a murderous life of its own. A story idea so absurd it takes someone as great at their craft as King to pull it off. In 1995 it was – not altogether successfully – turned into a movie directed by Tobe 'Yes, him again' Hooper.

His first novel concerned a teenage girl with telekinetic powers. Disappointed with it, he threw an early draft of it in the bin. It was Tabitha who fished it out and encouraged him to finish it. The novel, *Carrie*, was published in 1973 and while the initial hardback advance was relatively small, the paperback rights earned him enough to quit teaching and start writing full time. From reinventing the vampire in *Salem's Lot*, blowing away the Gothic cobwebs and planting them in middle America, to tales of a possessed automobile in *Christine*, from charting the apocalypse in *The Stand* to revisiting the assassination of John F. Kennedy in *11.22.63*, King has kept a little corner of our bookstore dark, weathering the highs and lows of commercial favour towards the horror genre.

He's even survived a brush with death himself. In 1999 he was walking along Maine State Route 5 in Lovell, Maine when Bryan Edwin Smith, looking away from the road to restrain his dog, hit King. The author was very badly injured, needing several operations and extensive physiotherapy. Like all good authors, he simply took the incident and fed it into his work.

His epic Dark Tower series features an alternative version of himself as a character – interestingly, a less than flattering one – and the need for the books' heroes Roland Deschain and Jake Chambers to save the author from the accident becomes a plot point. Nothing ever gets wasted in the life of an author, it's all just food for the stories.

At the time of writing he has gone on to complete a further fifty-four novels and several short story collections as well as screenplays for both movies and TV and several non-fiction projects.[16]

We haven't time to discuss them all, as much as I'd happily take the challenge on until you begged me to stop. So let's just look at the handful of titles that are especially linked to *Stranger Things*.

IT

Originally published in September 1986, King's book concerns a group of friends who, when they were children, fought a monstrous creature that was preying on kids in their home town of Derry. They thought they'd killed the beast, but a recent resurgence of deaths proves it's returned. Now, they have to reunite to finish off what they began twenty-eight years before.

It's a massive book, the UK paperback edition running to 1,116 pages.[17] But to suggest it's large purely in its physical mass is to undersell the sheer scope of the book. Flitting between some of the most perfect – and perfectly terrifying – evocations of childhood and the way our past comes back to haunt us, I would suggest it's King's masterwork, were it not for the fact that he's written so many great novels I can't actually make up my mind. Sorry.

---

16   Including 2000's *On Writing: A Memoir of the Craft*, which manages to be both a beautifully written memoir of King's life and a solid guide on the craft of writing that should certainly be read by anyone with an interest in taking up the dangerous habit.

17   The hardback first edition, which I keep on a specially strengthened bookshelf, only to be brought out should I need to actually stun a passing rhinoceros, runs to 912.

The Losers Club, the gang of children and later adults who are our heroes, are united as much by the fact that they're outsiders (bullied both at school and, in the case of a couple of them, at home too) as they are by shared interests. No dungeons and dragons here, but horror cinema looms large in their shared devotions. The childhood sections of the book are set, for the most part, during the summer of 1958 and the shadows of such glorious cinematic monsters as the *Creature from the Black Lagoon* and the tufty menace of Michael Landon's lycanthropic turn in *I was a Teenage Werewolf* loom large.[18] Although in all cases what they're seeing is the 'It' of the title, a creature that can become your worst nightmare, though it spends much of its time as Mr Bob Gray, otherwise known as Pennywise the Clown.

The Duffer Brothers first read the novel when they were the same age as the members of the Losers Club (early teens) and so the book had an extra resonance. Now, of course, like the Losers Club themselves, they have returned thirty years later to embrace the horror. Indeed, they tried to do so quite literally, having pitched to direct a movie of the

18   Yes really, high school troublemaker Tony Rivers is turned into a monster via regressive hypnotherapy. The movie's popularity led not only to eighties comedy *Teen Wolf* starring Michael J. Fox (which swaps the machinations of a villainous psychiatrist for a family curse) but also a slew of cash-ins. *I Was a Teenage Frankenstein* was at least brazen enough to acknowledge its obvious debt right there in the title; the same year's *Blood of Dracula*, while offering an identical plot but with fangs swapped for hair and claws, was a little more circumspect about it.

novel before they worked on *Stranger Things.*[19]

FIRESTARTER

While *Carrie* brought us a girl with telekinetic powers, it's in his 1980 novel that we see more of the compost from which *Stranger Things* will one day grow.

The novel tells the story of Andy and Charlie McGee, father and daughter, on the run from the (fictional … we hope) U.S. Department of Scientific Intelligence, colloquially known as The Shop. While at college, Andy and his girlfriend Victoria took part in an experiment conducted by The Shop, ingesting a hallucinogenic drug known as Lot 6 which imbued them with psychic powers. Andy has 'the push', an ability to control people with his mind, and Victoria became mildly telekinetic. But the drug lived on in their DNA and their daughter has a far more explosive power: she's pyrokinetic, able to cause fires with her mind.

The novel follows The Shop's attempts to capture Andy and Charlie, desperate to claim, and control, their powers for themselves.

---

19   During their August 2016 interview with *The Hollywood Reporter*, Matt states, "We asked, and that's why we ended up doing this [*Stranger Things*] because we'd asked Warner Brothers. I was like, 'Please,' and they were like, 'No.'" This was before Cary Fukunaga, the director of *Sin Nombre* (2009), *Jane Eyre* (2011), *Beasts of No Nation* (2015) and the jaw-droppingly wonderful TV series *True Detective* (2014), was brought on board. Then left again. The movie is now being helmed by Andrés Muschietti, director and co-writer of 2013's *Mama*. Finn Wolfhard is on board to play Richie Tozier, a member of the Losers Club. Indeed, he always was and if the initial adaptation had gone ahead as scheduled, he wouldn't have been able to appear in *Stranger Things*.

The book was later made into a movie with a young Drew Barrymore (two years after her appearance in *E.T. The Extra-Terrestrial*)[20] as the cute kid who can burn people alive with a thought.

Naturally, the notion of a secret government department dabbling in the creation of human monsters is something that lies at the heart of *Stranger Things*. Not that the idea of government conspiracies can entirely be claimed to be the creation of King, in fact there's no doubt that groups like The Shop have existed in countries all over the globe (see The Truth is Out There on page 140). Still, the book was clearly a touchstone for the show.

THE BODY

King's novella concerns a group of teenaged boys, all from troubled families, making a trip to find the corpse of a missing child. Originally published alongside three other novellas in the book *Different Seasons*, it's arguably more well known in its movie form, *Stand By Me*.[21] The 1986

---

20 And one year before her role in yet another Stephen King movie, *Cat's Eye*. King himself wrote the screenplay for this one, a portmanteau movie of three stories linked by the presence of a tabby cat (who becomes the most adorable hero of the third and final story, where he saves Drew Barrymore from a breath-stealing troll. I know, I know, like all good things it sounds absurd when reduced to a sentence, but give it a go, it's great fun).

21 As is one of the other novellas in the book: 'Rita Hayworth and Shawshank Redemption', which lost the 'Rita Hayworth' but gained seven Oscar nominations when written and directed by Fran Darabont in 1994. 'Apt Pupil', another novella in the book, was also adapted for the screen, directed by Bryan Singer and starring Sir Ian McKellen. In fact it's only the fourth – and most traditionally horrific – story, 'Breathing Method', that hasn't been pulled from *Different Seasons*'s pages and slapped on a screen.

movie adaptation, from director Rob Reiner, was one of a handful of movies that the Duffer Brothers recommended to their young cast for background viewing and, as previously mentioned, scenes from it were used as audition scripts.

You can see why a story of boys growing up to be men in the face of adversity – in the case of *Stand By Me*, the troubles of the road and bullies young and old – is a perfect sketch of the sort of group dynamic the Duffers wanted to bring to their young leads. Like the Losers Club before it, the bond between Gordie, Chris, Teddy and Vern is, in both the original novella and the movie, a perfect study of a young, cast-iron friendship (that, as with most cast-iron friendships we have in our youth, will dissipate to nothing within a few years of growing up).

GOLDEN YEARS

Not a novel but a 1991 TV mini-series written by King.[22] It concerns an elderly janitor who becomes caught up in the fallout of a secret government experiment. He finds he's miraculously getting younger but with operatives of The Shop on his trail he may not live long enough to enjoy it.

---

22 For the most part, he scripted the first five episodes and outlined the final two.

Like much of King's work on television in the nineties,[23] *Golden Years* offers mixed pleasures, not helped by the fact that it comes to a rather abrupt and unfulfilling end. The hope had been that the series would continue beyond the eight episodes but the network (CBS) decided not to renew their option. Home video releases – often trimmed to four hours – alter the ending so it appears to have at least a minimal resolution.

So, far from essential King, then, but given its themes it would be remiss not to mention it.

---

23   Given the length of his novels, King often found himself adapted into TV mini-series (frequently writing the scripts himself) but, while some of them are fondly remembered – particularly *It* (1990) and *The Stand* (1994) – the limitations of TV at the time frequently end up in them being somewhat flawed. The best, in my opinion anyway, and I'm the boss here in this footnote, is 1999's *Storm of the Century*, another original work scripted by King.

HOMEWORK

Well, you really need to read some Stephen King, don't you? I'll allow you to skip *Golden Years* but the other three are essential.

THINGS TO MAKE AND DO

Well, we've done a fair bit of heavy lifting so far haven't we? And I've given you a lot of homework so you deserve a break. Let's do something fun, let's make an Upside Down Cake!

INGREDIENTS

- 113G UNSALTED BUTTER (WHICH YOU WILL MELT)
- 113G UNSALTED BUTTER (WHICH YOU WON'T MELT)
- 183G BROWN SUGAR
- 134G WHITE SUGAR
- 192G PLAIN FLOUR
- 180ML MILK
- 2 EGGS
- 'SOME' FRESH PINEAPPLE PEELED, CORED AND CUT INTO CHUNKS OF ABOUT AN INCH[24]
- SOME GLACÉ CHERRIES (A HANDFUL, JUST ENOUGH TO THROW AWAY BECAUSE GLACÉ CHERRIES ARE THE DEVIL'S NIPPLES AND SHOULD NEVER BE USED)
- 1 ½ TEASPOONS BAKING POWDER
- ½ TEASPOON SALT
- ½ TEASPOON GROUND CINNAMON

---

24 Look, I can't do everything for you, you'll need enough to cover the entire top of the cake which is going to be about 20cm in diameter. This will take 'some' chunks. Just load it up and then feed the rest to a passing monkey.

LET'S GET ON WITH IT

IF YOU'RE THE sort of cook who gets stressed, first locate your bottle of wine. If not, then simply preheat your oven to 175°C (350°F).

IN A BOWL stir together the melted butter and the brown sugar and then spread the naughty mush evenly over the bottom of a well-greased cake tray (of about 20cm in diameter). Now take your 'some' pineapple, dry it off as much as you can using paper towels and then lay it evenly over the heart attack of butter and sugar.

NOW, WITH THE sort of unerring smugness that can only come from not having gone wrong yet, sift the flour, baking powder, salt and cinnamon together to form a super team of powdery goodness.

TAKE A LARGE mixing bowl, blend the unmelted butter with the white sugar until it's light and fluffy. To begin with this will seem like I have asked you to stir wood but as the butter warms up all will be well.

ADD THE EGGS, one at a time, beating after each.

STIR IN THE vanilla.

NOW WE ADD both the flour and milk – WAIT … I haven't finished, you do it like this: add the flour in three parts, alternating with the milk. Flour first, half of the milk, another third of the flour, rest of the milk, final third of the flour. Beat the mixture well after each new addition. If I am patronising you by being this methodical then forgive me, but I have enough problems in my life without avoiding the psychotic attentions of *Stranger Things* fans covered in the remains of a shit cake.

TAKE A MOMENT to just stand there, mixing bowl crooked in your arm, whisking away, feeling like a proper chef. Maybe even casually walk around the house so other people – or pets – see you, perhaps casually muttering, "Oh hi, just making one of my cakes, you know like I often do."

WHEN YOU'RE FEELING really full of yourself, spread the mix over what's already in your cake tray.

PUT THE CAKE-TO-BE in the oven and bake for about 45 to 55 minutes. What you're looking for is that perfect midway point between liquid and charcoal. If you're unsure, stick a skewer or something into it, when the skewer comes out clean rather than covered in goo, your cake's done.

LET THE CAKE cool on a baking rack (or the wire shelf taken from the oven if you're not Mary Berry, surrounded by all the kit) for about quarter of an hour.

THIS IS THE point at which you might completely ruin your cake (or discover you really didn't grease your tray well enough). You need to run a thin knife around the edge and then tip the cake out, turning it upside down so the pineapple is on top.

FOR THE OPTIMUM *Stranger Things* cake-eating experience, take the cake to some woods and eat it while screaming.

OR YOU CAN just have a slice while you read the next bit.

CHAPTER
TWO

THE WEIRDO
ON MAPLE STREET

W e return to Hawkins with the portentous rumble of thunder and the flash of lightning. It's the sort of night in which horror movies offer horrible faces at wet windows. A night to hide monsters. Perhaps even a night in which to make one. If a vacant lab at the Hawkins National Laboratory were to be allocated to a Doctor v. Frankenstein ("I'll need lots of conductive metal, some nice, bubbly chemicals, and a decent spade") we could hardly be surprised.

But the monsters can wait, because for now we have the quiet, cautious Eleven, in the care of Mike, Dustin and Lucas (though at times it will certainly be the other way around). Mike is gently smitten, Lucas doesn't trust her an inch and Dustin … well, Dustin simply can't believe he nearly saw her naked.

Meanwhile, Joyce is crumbling as Jonathan – poor, ever-dependable Jonathan – tries to keep the household afloat. And, in the woods, Hopper is dishing out sour looks and a few cautious dollops of backstory as the hunt for Will Byers continues.

The second chapter of our eight episode novel gives us space to get to know our characters a little more. Clearly, the main focus is the burgeoning trust between Mike and Eleven (and yes, here she gets to sample her first Eggo waffle, alongside, I'm sure, a copious quantity of pocket fluff).[1] From the terrible memories brought on by being trapped in the

---

1   While the boys later present Eleven with Mike's mum's meatloaf on a plate, we can only guess what grubby hiding places they might have used to smuggle it from the dinner table.

dark of Mike's closet ("Poppa!") to the surprised delight that only a suddenly unfolding recliner chair can bring, we are slowly getting inside Eleven's head. It's to Millie Bobby Brown's continued credit that we're with her every step of the way. Her performance is so delicate, so believable, that we cannot help but smile when she does, wince when she does, fear when she does.

But other relationships are developing too. Nancy has a party to go to ("Is that a new bra?" "No.") and we have our first sense that Steve may have competition for her affection. True, when Nancy approaches Jonathan as he pins up a 'missing' poster in the high school foyer, it's through a sense of empathy and kindness – two qualities Steve's friends clearly lack, what a slappable pair Tommy and Carol are – but Jonathan's utter, terrible awkwardness in her presence tells tales that his later scenes, photographing her from the shadows of the woods, only deepen.

We finally meet the Byers boys' father too, louche Lonnie with his young girlfriend and his pathetic attempts to playact the role of a father. Jonathan is old enough and wise enough to know he's better off without him, poor young Will less so. Of course, Will has more immediate problems, as Eleven illustrates with the aid of some D & D miniatures and the game board.[2]

But let's talk about Barb.

What is it about Barb?

WHY ARE WE ALL SO OBSESSED BY BARB?

---

2   "Wait, so … he's hiding under some wood? Under the table maybe? Erm … You will help me pick all my miniatures up, won't you?"

Let me play devil's advocate for a moment; bear with me and try not to throw the book across the room. Yes, so Barb is a nice enough friend. But she's a tad preachy, don't you think? OK, it's clear she doesn't like or trust Steve and, on the evidence she gets to see I suppose we can't entirely blame her. He has lousy, mean spirited friends, he thinks drinking a can of beer from a hole is cool and … well, who knows what else she's seen that we're not privy to? Still, it's also clear that one of Barb's main concerns is that if Nancy ends up becoming part of Steve's group she'll end up losing her friend. It's a selfish motivation – hoping her best friend's relationship tanks so she can keep her for herself – but it's understandable that it would worry her. We'd like to think we'd rise above such selfishness, that we'd be happy for Nancy and never mind that all those nights we used to have fun, we're now on our own because STEVE. But would we?

When it comes to the end of the party and Nancy and Barb have their moment in Steve's hallway, Nancy – halfway towards Steve's bedroom in more ways than one – tells Barb to go home. Let's give Barb the benefit of the doubt, she's worried her friend is about to do something she'll later regret. Her disapproval is for the best of reasons. Yes, let's assume that. But her, "This isn't you …" seems, I don't know … harsh? If she'd said, "Are you sure?" or, "I don't think this is a good idea," then, OK, that's friendly support. That's concern. But … "This isn't you?" It isn't Nancy to be attracted to Steve? To want to sleep with him? Who made Barb mum all of a sudden? I don't blame Nancy for losing her friendliness for a moment and becoming more insistent that Barb should just go home.

Perhaps I'm being harsh. Barb clearly doesn't decide to just leave, she sits on the diving board and waits for her friend. It would have been better had she not.

I wonder though, if the main reason we like her is that many of us recognise a little of ourselves in her?[3] She's the female equivalent of Mike, Lucas, Dustin and Will, she's the outsider, the one with limited friends who would never have been invited to this party normally. She is, to put it simply, the geek. Like us. Oh come on, you're reading this and I'm writing it, we can admit it. Hell, we can be proud of it. So is that why we love her? Certainly the Duffer Brothers related easily to her as they admitted in their interview with *The Daily Beast*: "High school was terrible for us," Ross Duffer told journalist Melissa Leon. "We both hated it and just felt very much outside the whole time, looking in. Let's just put it this way: it was not difficult to write the Barb character.

FAMILIAR THINGS

You Have Entered the Fifth Dimension

"MAPLE STREET, U.S.A. LATE SUMMER. A TREE-LINED LITTLE WORLD OF FRONT PORCH GLIDERS, BARBECUES, THE LAUGHTER OF CHILDREN AND THE BELL OF AN ICE-CREAM VENDOR. AT THE SOUND OF THE ROAR AND THE FLASH OF LIGHT, IT WILL BE PRECISELY 6:43 P.M. ON MAPLE STREET. THIS IS MAPLE STREET ON A

---

3   Not me, obviously, I was always the cool kid at school. Yeah. I had so many friends it was embarrassing. I was Steve. Definitely. What? Stop laughing! All of the people that knew me as a kid, STOP LAUGHING.

LATE SATURDAY AFTERNOON. MAPLE STREET – IN THE LAST CALM
AND REFLECTIVE MOMENT – BEFORE THE MONSTERS CAME."

Opening Narration to 'The Monsters are Due On Maple Street',
The Twilight Zone, 1960

The first reference we come to is actually in the title of the episode itself. Of course, it could be a coincidence but, if so, I suggest the Duffer Brothers do what every creative does when someone sees something in their work that they didn't intend to be there: Nod wisely and say, "Cool, you spotted that huh?"

'The Monsters are Due on Maple Street' is an episode from the first season of TV series *The Twilight Zone*,[4] often regarded as one of the finest episodes of the original run.[5] A story of suburban paranoia, residents of Maple Street start to become hostile and suspicious after a passing meteor causes a power failure. The episode was written by the show's creator (and narrator) Rod Serling.

Fear Addicted, Danger Illustrated

While I've already talked about the links between *Stranger Things*' Eleven and Stephen King's sparky Charlie McGee, it's worth pointing out that both characters get nosebleeds when they use their powers. Of course, it's become a

---

4   For more on the series see my movie recommendations – yes, I actually ended up giving in and writing a whole damn list of them – at the end of the book.

5   Indeed, *Time* magazine included it in their list of the top ten episodes of the show in a 2009 feature.

common trope in TV and cinema to illustrate the internal strain and damage caused by wielding such 'gifts'. David Cronenberg's *Scanners* had it worse: the longer they used their mental powers the more damage their bodies endured, veins popping to the surface and beginning to leak.

THEY'RE HERE

Another solid *Poltergeist* reference, with Joyce Byers craning to hear the otherworldly voice on her new telephone. In *Poltergeist*, the phone – and the television, amidst a hiss of white noise – brought the voices of the dead.

POSTER DOUBLE

Horror thrillers have made a habit of a hero witnessing something they didn't mean to. Michelangelo Antonioni's *Blow Up*, Dario Argento's *Profondo Rosso*,[6] Alfred Hitchcock's *Rear Window*, even Agatha Christie's glorious *The 4.50 from Paddington*, where an old lady on a train sees someone being strangled in another train as it passes. Brian De Palma (who also directed the 1976 adaptation of Stephen King's *Carrie*) used the trope a couple of times but it's in his 1984 movie, *Body Double*, where we find a solid link with this scene. The

---

6   Which gets bonus points. In the movie, the hero (David Hemmings, who played a similar role in *Blow Up*) sees someone being murdered in an upstairs window. He runs to intervene but he's too late. As is common in these movies, he spends the rest of the movie convinced he saw something of importance. He did and, Argento, being a terribly clever boy, lets the audience see it too, we just don't notice. Watch the movie to the end, then reverse and pause the scene in question, you'll be terribly impressed.

hero in De Palma's movie voyeuristically watches a woman he's attracted to as she strips behind a venetian-blinded window. The visual parallels between De Palma's movie (most particularly its poster) and Jonathan, the peeping-tom who ends up photographing Barb's fate, are close enough that I can't help but point them out.

BLOOD IN THE WATER

The Duffer Brothers told Mark Steger, the dancer, choreographer and actor inside the Demogorgon monster suit, that he should think of the monster he's playing as being like the shark in *Jaws*. Never is that endorsed more on screen than in the monster's ability to scent blood. The droplets, dissipating in the cool blue water of Jonathan's swimming pool after Barb cuts her hand, couldn't nod to Spielberg's movie more without strapping on a dorsal fin and singing John Williams's famous score at the top of its voice.

STRANGER SOUNDS

So what do we find on the jukebox for the second episode of *Stranger Things*? Time travel. That's what. But we'll get that in due course; in fact I've travelled back in time from a later paragraph right now, in order to prove such things are possible.

The song that carries a good deal of the emotional weight is 'Should I Stay or Should I Go' by English punk band The Clash. Jonathan hears the song on the car radio while driving to see if Will is with his father, and he's then reminded of the time he played Will the song. Of course, we'll hear it again throughout the series.

Formed in 1976, The Clash were part of the original wave of British punk. The song itself is certainly one of their most commercially successful, though its greatest success was when it was re-released in 1991 on the back of its inclusion in a commercial for Levi's jeans. Which isn't terribly punk but there you go. It went to number one in the UK charts.

The backing vocals are sung in Ecuadorian Spanish for no good reason whatsoever. Guitarist Joe Strummer decided it would be fun, so the tape operator in the studio, Eddie Garcia – who was Ecuadorian – telephoned his mother for help in translating the lyrics.

In 2012, pubescent pop sound-makers One Direction received considerable flak after their single 'Live While We're Young' appropriated the opening riff to the The Clash song.[7] Band-member and troubler of female hormones, Harry Styles, didn't help matters when he told an interviewer for BBC Newsbeat, "It was kind of on purpose though, it's a great riff ..." That's alright then, Harry, as long as you like it. Kids today, they're always stealing music.

Also in Jonathan's car we hear '(You're A) Go Nowhere' by Reagan Youth, another punk band, this time hailing from America. The song comes from their first album, *Youth Anthems for the New Order*, which wasn't actually released until 1984, a year after *Stranger Things* is set.

Perhaps it's Jonathan's car that travels in time because,

---

7   Completely bloody nicked.

by the time he arrives at his father's house, he's able to hear Lonnie and girlfriend Cynthia watch the video for 'I'm Taking Off (Shield Your Eyes)' on the TV. The song is by Space Knife, the tongue in cheek creation of 'Bruce Knife'.[8] While it's clearly designed as a homage to eighties synth pop, it was actually released in 2013. The song can be downloaded for free from Space Knife's Bandcamp page as part of their first – and, at the time of writing, only – release, a three track EP entitled *Space Knife Greatest Hits Volume One*.

For a little seasonal cheer, we hear some Christmas favourites tinkling away between the aisles of Melvald's General Store. First that jaunty anthem of festive home improvement, 'Deck the Halls' performed by Chicks With Hits, a female duo based in Brighton UK whose work is frequently licensed for TV and movie use. Then, while Joyce is charmingly breaking her boss's wallet, we hear 'Jingle Bells' sung by The Canterbury Choir.

But enough of Christmas! We have a party to go to!

When Steve greets Nancy and Barb we hear the singularly appropriate 'Raise A Little Hell' from Canadian rockers Trooper. Later, our wild young things decide drinking beer normally is too much fuss, it's much nicer to almost choke to death on it using physics and a knife. During this act of liquid stupidity, we hear the sound of UK new wave band Modern

---

8   The bio on Space Knife's Bandcamp page reads: "No one knows when Bruce Knife was born but everyone remembers their first time to hear his band, Space Knife. His musical experimentation combined with the serenity in his voice gave Space Knife a sound like no other. With many #1 hits and platinum-selling albums his fan base grew to the millions." The page also claims that his career has had many ups and downs but that we should not expect any less from a man as complicated as Bruce. https://spaceknife.bandcamp.com

English and their song 'I Melt With You'. "I saw the world thrashing all around your face," go the lyrics. "No, that's not the world, that's an exploding can of really horrible cheap beer. Steve, you're a show-off, fetch me a vodka and tonic and get over yourself."

Founded in the cradle of all things edgy and rebellious, Colchester, Essex, Modern English recorded and released four albums in the eighties before entering a cycle of disbanding and reuniting again to release four more. Their latest, *Take Me to the Trees*, came out in 2016.

According to singer, Robbie Grey, 'I Melt With You' is about a couple having sex while nuclear bombs fall. As well you might.

Finally, as Steve and Nancy prepare to make love and poor Barb sits on the diving board of Probably Be Dead in a Minute, we travel in time again for one more song. When selecting a track that would perfectly accompany the spilling of bodily fluid and the satiating of savage hunger (as well as the fate of poor Barb) the production team went for the 1987 cover version of Simon and Garfunkel's 'Hazy Shade of Winter' performed by The Bangles.

The Bangles were an American female rock trio, famous for their hits 'Walk Like an Egyptian', 'Eternal Flame' and 'Manic Monday'. Unless you were a hormonal teenage male,[9] in which case they were famous for Susanna Hoffs.

---

9   Tautology, noun (plural tautologies): The saying of the same thing twice over in different words, generally considered to be a fault of style.

HONOURABLE STRANGERS

Who do we find on the roll-call of honourable guest cast to be mentioned this episode? Well, it's a bit of a cheat because, strictly speaking, they're recurring cast members who are being included simply because they're not on the list of cast members elsewhere. Yes folks! Proffer those wrists for the handcuffs, it's Rob Morgan and John Paul Reynolds, otherwise known as Officers Powell and Callaghan.

Rob Morgan has served his time, as all actors must, in small roles in TV shows and movies. It's part of an actor's job to turn up at Oh My God O'Clock in the morning for the joy of playing 'Third Homeless Man' or 'Angry Customer' while their career gets on its feet.[10] He soon graduated to meatier roles on shows such as 2014's *Believe* and *The Knick*. 2016 sees two roles vie for the coveted position of 'probably most well known for':[11] our very own Officer Powell, or long-suffering criminal/snitch Turk in Netflix's Marvel shows *Daredevil* and *Luke Cage*.

The year 2016 has also been busy for John Paul Reynolds (or simply John Reynolds, as he's usually credited). As well as *Stranger Things* he appeared in the comedy *Thanksgiving*, a show that evolves in real time showing the Morgan family's dysfunctional Thanksgiving celebration. He also stars in *Search Party*, a dark comedy about a group of friends who set out to find a missing college acquaintance. A second series was green lit by the TBS channel at the end of 2016.

---

10   I have entirely invented these roles, stop Googling them.

11   By lazy writers.

NOTES

HOMEWORK

Time once more to tax your knowledge
of the infuriatingly obscure![12]

1. Where does Lucas think Eleven may have escaped from? (And I want a specific name, not just a general term)

2. When it's suggested Eleven might be a 'psycho' who is the cinematic example Dustin immediately thinks of and what film franchise do they appear in?

3. How big is Mike's family's TV set?

4. Mike's dad allegedly spends most of his time sleeping in what?

5. What brand of cigarette does Joyce smoke?

6. Mike shows Eleven the figure of which Star Wars character?

7. What is the name of Mike's toy dinosaur?

8. The school holds a special assembly on the football field because of Will's disappearance. What time is it scheduled to start?

9. What year did the last person go missing in Hawkins, Indiana?

10. And when was the last suicide?

ADDITIONAL RESEARCH

Watch at least three episodes of *The Twilight Zone*. Even better, pick up the first season on Blu-ray where it positively glows with gorgeousness.

---

12 Or just make you really cross.

NOTES

THE DNA OF STRANGER THINGS – STEVEN SPIELBERG

When Andrew Liptak, writer and critic, said of *Stranger Things*, "It's basically an eight-hour version of a Steve Spielberg movie,"[13] he was being intentionally reductive. Still, there's no doubting the influence that Spielberg's work, most particularly *Jaws*, *Close Encounters of the Third Kind*, *E.T. The Extra-Terrestrial* and *Poltergeist*, had on the Duffer Brothers and their show.

He is the highest-grossing director in history and has a career in cinema spanning thirty movies and forty-five years.[14]

His love of cinema was, like that of the Duffer Brothers, obvious from when he was young; like them he was making home movies by the age of twelve.

As a student, he accepted an unpaid internship in Universal Studios' editing department. While there he made a short film, *Amblin'*,[15] which won several awards and led Sidney Sheinberg, vice president of Universal, to offer him a seven-year directing contract. Spielberg, at twenty-one, was the youngest director ever to be offered such a contract.

---

13 On Wired.com's Geek's Guide to the Galaxy podcast.

14 According to number-crunching from website Boxofficemojo.com. Interestingly, the top slots are all held by directors predominantly known for sci-fi and fantasy. The number-two slot (appropriately *coughs politely*) is held by Michael Bay, with Peter Jackson coming third, Robert Zemeckis fourth and James Cameron fifth.

15 The title of which, minus the apostrophe, he later used as the name of his production company.

He dropped out of college (though later returned to finish his degree) and directed a number of TV shows for Universal, most significantly part of the pilot episode of *Night Gallery*, the horror anthology show from Rod Serling, the creator of *The Twilight Zone*.[16]

While Spielberg was overjoyed to be living his dream as a director, he found himself on the receiving end of a good deal of hostility due to his young age, later telling author Peter Biskind for his book *Easy Riders Raging Bulls*: "I had everybody on the set against me. The average age of the crew was sixty years old. When they saw me walk on the stage, looking younger than I really was, like a baby, everybody turned their back on me, just walked away. I got the sense that I represented this threat to everyone's job." In a sense he – and other new talents like him – did. The seventies were a landmark decade for Hollywood. The old studio system, where the producer was king, was changing. It was the decade of the auteur; young directors – such as Martin Scorsese, Francis Ford Coppola, William Friedkin, Peter Bogdanovich and, of course, Spielberg himself – shook up how movies were made. The director ruled.[17]

---

16   The pilot for *Night Gallery* was, in effect, a full-length movie composed of three horror stories. Spielberg directed the central segment, a typical Rod Serling, twist-in-the-tail piece concerning an unpleasant, blind millionairess who pays a down-on-his-luck gambler nine thousand dollars for his eyes. SPOILER WARNING: A surgeon transplants them into the woman, warning her that the sight she gains will only be temporary. Seconds after opening her new eyes, there's a blackout and she can't see a thing.

17   Albeit briefly. The system was to change again – for all but the proven talents who had the clout to get their way – and return to the more studio-led world of movies we have today. The movie often credited for bringing the period of directorial control to an end was *Heaven's Gate*, the 1980 movie from Michael Cimino, which bombed so appallingly it bankrupted its studio.

In 1971, Spielberg directed *Duel*, his first full-length movie.[18] A stunning piece of work, the thrilling story of a motorist being stalked by a huge tanker truck, scripted by Richard Matheson based on his own short story.[19]

A handful of other TV movies followed, plus his first cinema feature, *The Sugarland Express*, but it's with 1975's *Jaws* that Spielberg finally solidified his reputation as a director with a long and awesome career ahead of him.

Spielberg's tale of a naughty fish ruining everyone's holiday was based on the bestselling novel by Peter Benchley and became the highest grossing movie of all time, establishing the whole phenomenon of the summer blockbuster.[20]

Spielberg's next film, *Close Encounters of the Third Kind*, saw Spielberg reunite with *Jaws* star Richard Dreyfuss as he swaps fretting about sharks for fretting about aliens. When Winona Ryder starts unpacking the Christmas lights trying to contact her son, she is certainly channelling the spirit of *Close Encounters*, which features Melinda Dillon as a mother whose house is plagued by electrical disturbances and whose son is abducted by the aliens causing such. Dillon's character along with Dreyfuss's are two people, thought mad

---

18 Originally shot for TV, a longer cut was later released theatrically.

19 Richard Matheson is a legend in the world of sci-fi and horror, his short stories, novels and movie scripts are a profound influence on many modern-day writers (including Stephen King who cites him as his most major influence). He is perhaps most well known for his novel *I Am Legend* but his CV is so long and illustrious it's merely one glowing entry amongst a whole sky of stars.

20 Not adjusting the box-office receipts for inflation, it would hold the record until *Star Wars* beat it in 1977.

by friends and family alike, who pursue their gut instinct – and hallucinations of a mountain, which Dreyfuss sculpts out of mashed potato in one of the movie's most pleasingly nuts moments – to communicate with the aliens they know are out there.

The movie had a relatively long gestation. Spielberg had wanted to do direct a sci-fi picture for some time. Indeed, had actually already done so. At the age of seventeen he made the movie *Firelight,* a tale of scientists investigating UFO sightings, on a budget of $500. Spielberg composed the soundtrack to the movie on his clarinet, which his mother (a pianist) then transposed to sheet music so his high school band could play it. The movie was shown at his local movie theatre and netted him a profit of one dollar. Several shots and ideas from *Firelight* would make their way into *Close Encounters.*

After rejecting several scripts for the film, Spielberg wrote it with screenwriter Jerry Nelson. The production was rushed and Spielberg was dissatisfied with elements of the version initially released. This led to two further versions being produced over the years: initially, in 1980, a 'Special Edition' which added several scenes, including material set inside the aliens' ship at the end. This latter was at the studio's insistence who felt it would add commercial value to a reissue. Spielberg cut them all out again for the third, and arguably definitive, version prepared for home video in 1998.

After a sidestep into wartime comedy with 1979's *1941*[21] and grave-robbing, whip-enthusiast Indiana Jones in 1981's

---

21   The author would like to formally apologise for this sentence.

Raiders of the Lost Ark, Spielberg made another movie which flavours *Stranger Things* more than a tad.

E.T. The Extra-Terrestrial saw Spielberg once more gazing towards the stars. Though, in a sense, he was gazing far more into himself. When his parents divorced in 1960, the fourteen-year-old Spielberg invented an imaginary alien friend. That friend, as with Elliot, the young character at the heart of the movie, filled the gap left by his father.

Indeed, Elliot is very much Spielberg as a child (including his trick of feigning illness by holding a thermometer to a lightbulb and passing off the high temperature as a fever) and the growing bond between Elliot and the friendly alien he takes under his wing finds its parallel in the relationship between Mike and Eleven.[22]

This is never more explicit – and the reference is, of course, intentional – when Eleven is dressed up in a blonde wig and girls' clothes. In the movie Elliot and his brother Michael disguise E.T. as their younger sister,[23] in order to get him out of the house.

The movie was another huge success for Spielberg, once again becoming the highest grossing film of all time, a record it would hold until it was beaten in 1993 by a movie about a theme park that goes awry, *Jurassic Park*, also

---

22   Although, for the record, ET never kisses Elliot and, no matter how many times I watch the movie I simply can't pretend there's a sexual attraction between Elliot and his long-necked, glowing-fingered friend from the stars.

23   Although their real sister is, of course, played by Drew Barrymore, who got the role thanks to her brazen lying during her audition, the six-year-old insisting to Spielberg that she wasn't an actress at all but was, in fact, the drummer for a punk band called the Purple People Eaters. Spielberg couldn't resist such a fertile imagination and hired her.

directed by Spielberg. Show-off.

POLTERGEIST
While Spielberg was preparing *E.T. The Extra-Terrestrial*,[24]
a clause in his contract stipulated that he wasn't allowed
to direct another film. Which was awkward, as he had one
he want to direct, a horror movie about a family besieged
by ghosts. Tobe Hooper, who had made his name with the
groundbreaking low-budget picture *The Texas Chain Saw
Massacre*, was brought on as director[25] with Spielberg co-
producing the film alongside Frank Marshall,[26] working from
a script whose birth is certainly complex but inarguably has

---

24   During the shooting of these scenes, Spielberg apparently dressed up in
     wig and cardigan himself and went trick or treating with the cast after the
     shoot.

25   Though it's been an ongoing debate how much of the movie he actually
     did direct. So much so, in fact, that an investigation was opened by The
     Director's Guild of America (with the concern being for Hooper's reputation).
     Reports vary and there's little doubt that Spielberg – on set for the vast
     majority of the shoot – will certainly have made his presence felt. Hooper
     however insists that while Spielberg certainly directed some second unit
     shots and worked on some of the storyboards, the film was his.

26   Frank Marshall co-founded Amblin Entertainment with his wife Kathleen
     Kennedy and Spielberg. His name is attached to many eighties sci-fi
     favourites such as the *Back to the Future* trilogy, **batteries not included*, the
     Indiana Jones movies and *Who Framed Roger Rabbit?*. Marshall is a keen
     magician, sometimes performing under the name Dr Fantasy. In *Poltergeist*,
     when the Freeling family evacuate their haunted house to take up residence
     in a nearby Holiday Inn, eagle-eyed viewers will spot a sign on the hotel
     hoarding saying 'Welcome Dr Fantasy & friends'.

Spielberg's fingerprints all over it.[27] The story of a house under siege from external forces – forces that steal that family's youngest child – certainly feeds into elements of *Stranger Things*.

Let's quickly kick the elephant out of the room: while there is a popular legend that suggests the *Poltergeist* movie was cursed (due to the death of four of the actors involved, two of whom died from long-suffered illnesses) it wasn't. I trust that's cleared that up.[28]

One final piece of Spielberg-related trivia: a scene in the movie requires one of the characters to tear off their own face (I know, I know, it's that kind of movie). The effects shot was so important, given it would have to be completed in a single take, that the hands you see on screen doing all the

---

27 *Deep breath* As mentioned in a footnote in the 'Real Things' section (page 34) John Sayles originally wrote a script for Spielberg entitled *Night Skies*, elements of which would end up being reused both in *E.T. The Extra-Terrestrial* and *Poltergeist*. It centred on a family besieged in their home by evil aliens. Tobe Hooper, who was lined up to direct that film, commented that he wasn't particularly interested in aliens and would like it more if the family were under threat from ghosts, although he would later go on to direct fifties B-movie homage *Invaders From Mars* and the deliriously fun *Lifeforce*. Spielberg wrote a new treatment (the title changed to *Night Time*) and Stephen King was approached to write the screenplay. King's agent asked for too much money, so the job instead went to Michael Grais and Mark Victor who, on seeing Tobe Hooper was attached, turned in a harrowing, 'full-on' horror screenplay (in which, for example, the young daughter Carol Anne was killed). Spielberg wasn't happy with it so rewrote the next draft himself with Frank Marshall and Kathleen Kennedy offering suggestions. So far so good. Though there is an added complication: it's suggested that a number of the story ideas were directly influenced by Richard Matheson, elements from *Hell House* and his *Twilight Zone* episode Little Girl Lost finding their way into the story. While Matheson didn't get a credit he was later hired by Spielberg to serve as creative consultant on the Spielberg produced TV show *Amazing Stories*, a job Matheson feels he was given as thanks for him not pursuing the matter.

28 No, *The Exorcist* wasn't cursed either. Shush.

tearing are Spielberg's own.

THE GOONIES

A movie that, along with *Stand By Me*, the Duffer Brothers gave to their young cast as an example of the bond they wanted Mike, Lucas, Will and Dustin to share. *The Goonies* involves a group of boys, the open, friendly Mikey,[29] inventive genius Data, loudmouth joker Mouth and the overweight Chunk. Together they get into a scrape involving not government agents and monsters, but a criminal family and stolen pirate treasure.

The story was written by Spielberg, who also executive produced, with the screenplay being handled by Chris Columbus.[30] The movie was directed by Richard Donner.

---

29 Walsh rather than Wheeler, but I'm betting I know where the Duffer Brothers got Mike's name from.

30 Columbus also wrote *Gremlins* (1984) and *Young Sherlock Holmes* (1985) for Amblin Entertainment and eventually became better known as a director, helming – amongst many other movies – the first two *Home Alone* pictures and the first two films in the *Harry Potter* franchise.

HOMEWORK

Naturally, if you haven't seen *Jaws, Close Encounters of the Third Kind, Alien The Alien*, [31] *Poltergeist* and *The Goonies* then you should, but I'm going to add *Duel* in there too because it's frankly wonderful and you'll thank me for insisting you watch it.

---

31 Yes, I am a bit tired of having to type *E.T. The Extra-Terrestrial*, how did you guess?

NOTES

CHAPTER THREE

HOLLY JOLLY

❝Nothing happened." Oh but Nancy, that's not entirely true now, is it?

We open in the Upside Down, where dust motes/feathers/snowflakes float in the air like particles in water. A nightmarish flip version of the real world. The here that lies just to the left. Poor Barb is in a drained swimming pool and soon fighting for her life, because – as we know only too well – this thick, liquid reality has a shark swimming in it and it's terribly, terribly hungry.

With our third episode the Duffer Brothers take a break from writing and directing. They're show runners so, naturally, they're hardly absent, but Shawn Levy[1] takes over the director's chair for this episode and the next – to allow the Duffer Brothers the space to concentrate on getting the rest of the series written – while the script is by Jessica Mecklenburg.[2] Naturally, given the show is a piece of an eight chapter novel, many viewers would be forgiven for not noticing.

Our world deepens; not only the dark underside that is the Upside Down, fleshed out a little more with each visit, but also the work of Dr Brenner and the unpleasant life of Eleven. Few can put their hands on their hips to look moody

---

1　See the 'Honourable Strangers' entry for the next episode.

2　Mecklenburg is also co-executive producer on the show (alongside Ian Paterson, who I simply must mention was also a producer on 1988's *Friday the 13th Part VII – The New Blood*, one of the more ridiculous – yet fun – entries in the franchise) and has written numerous TV screenplays including episodes of *Huff*, *Swingtown*, *Saving Grace* and *Being Mary Jane*.

in a protective suit – you may as well try and look suave in a onesie – but Mathew Modine gives it the sort of game effort that only a Mathew Modine can. We barely notice because we're too busy throwing things at the screen. If we were on the fence as to our opinion of Brenner (and, really, we shouldn't have been) this episode goes all out to paint him in villainous colours. He wants Eleven to kill a fluffy white cat and that is rarely applauded behaviour. He may as well have given her a baby meerkat and a hammer, we could hardly loathe him less. In fact I can't help but wonder if he's been moving up a psychological ladder of animal squishing. Did he start off with a particularly ugly spider? Or a dung beetle wearing a Ku Klux Klan hood? Surely you don't move straight from Coke cans to adorable, white fluffy things?

Thankfully, Eleven refuses. There's a limit to what she'll do to please her 'father'. Ultimately – awfully – he ends up being pleased with her anyway, a moment of tenderness we know is all too rare in Eleven's life, as he strokes her cheek and calls her incredible. And to think, all she had to do to earn such praise is snuff out the life of two human beings. There are times in all of our lives when we feel we don't quite live up to our parents' expectations of us; let us take solace from the fact that Martin Brenner isn't <u>our</u> Poppa.

From a dysfunctional 'parent' to a genuine and distraught one. Joyce Byers is getting more desperate by the moment, with only the audience aware that she is far from mad sitting in her Christmas fantasia of lights as we have given homage to on the cover. Now, let me risk a negative – albeit a personal one. In general, I am not a fan of dramatic conflict created by misunderstanding.[3] I hate that excruciating period of uncertainty where a character stands alone, misunderstood in their fictional world. At its worst – *The Walking Dead*, I'm looking at you – it's created by characters not speaking to one another, strutting off screen without explaining themselves properly so that false perceptions can breed like plot-sucking ticks in their absence. "Just explain!" you end up screaming at the screen.[4] "If one of you just opened your mouths and had a proper conversation this entire situation would be dealt with and we could move on to something more interesting!" I consider it the fictional equivalent of chewing on tinfoil.

In the case of Joyce, I accept it's relatively short-lived and entirely believable. Besides, Winona Ryder is doing her very best 'I'm A Bit Wobbly' acting and, were I in the position of having brought her a casserole, as poor Karen Wheeler has here, I would be speed dialling the local health authority while maintaining a fixed, terrified grin and making a mental note of where all the sharp knives were. Still, as a viewer, I will be gleeful once Joyce is acknowledged as the sane, loving (if, yes, somewhat highly strung and skittish) mother she really is.

---

3   There are no hard and fast rules in storytelling. None. So there is no such thing as a watertight opinion on what you should or should not do. So accept I'm making a very generalised point here and that I know full well there are countless times when my opinion would be wrongheaded in context.

4   Me. *I* would be shouting at the screen. I really shouldn't drag you into it, you may be the sort of sane person who doesn't have conversations with two-dimensional projections of fictional characters that exist neither in the real world nor, indeed, in your living room.

By the end of the episode we also have Eleven in the agonising position of being vilified for something she hasn't done. When she leads the boys to Will's house she was right on the money, that's where he is (albeit on the Upside Down) and Mike's anger when he decides she must have been lying all along … OH GOD.

Again, yes, believable and understandable … but roll on the moment when dramatic conflict built on false perception can fall away. It makes my fists clench something rotten. These lovely people have enough on their plate as it is without sniping at one another.[5] Give me conflict built on truth every time.

On the subject of truth, it's lovely to see Hopper so swiftly sniffing out the suspicious smell at the heart of Brenner's work. He may be a lousy date but he's proving to be a reliable policeman as he starts to probe deeper into the work being done on the town's doorstep. Should I ever vanish in mysterious circumstances,[6] I want Hopper on the case.

And as for Joyce's conversation with her son via the medium of Christmas lights – "Where are you?" RIGHT HERE "What should I do?" RUN – it's a delicious séance with a sparkle.

---

5   *Offers extra narrow-eyed stare at Lucas*

6   No doubt kidnapped by a fellow *Stranger Things* fan wanting me to apologise for including so many footnotes.

FAMILIAR THINGS

Very little in the way of overt references here (at least, not that I haven't already mentioned, yes there's a *Jaws* movie poster prominently on display but I can't talk about that EVERY time.) There is, however, one of particular note:

Shoot It In The Eye!

Lucas's wrist rocket (a slingshot, whatever he says) is another solid reference to Stephen King's *It* in which a slingshot proves to be a surprisingly effective weapon. As for shooting it in the eye and blinding it, another of Stephen King's young heroes, Marty Coslaw, does just that to the monster he must face in the novella 'Cycle of the Werewolf', and its movie adaptation *Silver Bullet* (1985).

Nostalgia

But we can certainly take the time to talk about the sheer wealth of eighties gorgeousness on view here, because this episode features even more than usual.

Steve, perhaps showing support for the Hawkins High School team, but most likely being the big-haired trend setter we all know he is, sports his Le Tigre polo shirt.

Le Tigre flaunts faux Frenchness; it's an American label that was designed to compete with the (genuinely French) Lacoste brand. A tiger leaps nobly over Steve's nipple in place of the crocodile found on Lacoste clothing. The brand became particularly successful during the eighties but fashion is fickle and ceased production during the nineties until a comeback in 2003.

Coca-Cola becomes the go-to drink for murdering people with your brain, as Eleven reminisces over the lovely time she crushed an empty can of it to please her Poppa. The retro advert is as likely to cause a sugar rush as the drink itself.

Also on the TV, Eleven catches a glimpse of *He-Man*, the animated series built on the back of a highly successful toy line (as many cartoons of the eighties were, *Transformers* anyone?). He-Man was the alter-ego of Prince Adam, who transformed – gaining a spray tan but losing some clothes – whenever he pointed his magic sword at the sky and yelled, "By the power of Grayskull!" There was an entertainingly awful movie adaptation in 1987, with He-Man portrayed by Swedish punch-machine Dolph Lundgren; there was also an early appearance by Courtney Cox. He-Man's nemesis, the skull-faced Skeletor, was played by the splendid Frank Langella.[7] At the end of the movie, he claws himself free of the bubbling pool of plot to announce, "I'll be back." He wasn't.

The original *He-Man* cartoon also offered a spin-off aimed at a female market, *She-Ra Princess of Power*. Maybe Eleven would have liked her better. Though I doubt it. Nobody did.

Finally, we get to see Ronald Reagan, former US President, briefly discussing the US plans for the 'Star Wars' defence

---

7   Whose CV includes a handful of juicy genre moments, from playing Eastern European jugular-botherer Dracula in 1979 to Detective Hayden in 1994's computer-game-killer horror movie *Brainscan*. He also appeared in *Cutthroat Island* alongside Mathew Modine.

program in a clip that at least helps to put Inspector Callaghan's assumptions about Dr Brenner's work into context.

STRANGER SOUNDS

"I've been waiting ... for a girl like you ... to chew on and drag into another dimension ..." as Foreigner never sang. Foreigner was the brainchild of English rockers Mick Jones and Ian McDonald and American Lou Gramm. They will always be remembered for their power ballads such as 'Waiting for a Girl Like You' (as heard here in the opening of the episode) and 'I Want to Know What Love Is'. Should you feel the need to clench angsty fists and shake your long hair while singing loudly in front of some flames, put some Foreigner on, it'll work a treat.

The other song prominently featured is a cover version of the David Bowie song "'Heroes'".[8] Bowie wrote the song while recording in Berlin in 1977, inspired by seeing his producer Tony Visconti kissing his girlfriend, the Berlin Wall behind them. The cover version is by Peter Gabriel, from his album *Scratch My Back*, a musical project where Gabriel recorded a number of his favourite songs (in stripped down orchestral versions) with the artists he covered then selecting one of Gabriel's songs to cover in return. *And I'll Scratch Yours*, the follow up album of people covering Gabriel songs, was released three years later.

---

8   Don't forget the quotation marks, there to denote irony; if you do, ardent Bowie fans – of which I am one – will sneer at you.

HONOURABLE STRANGERS

How can we not cast an appreciative glance at the splendid Christi Waldon who basks in her brief role as Marissa, the Hawkins librarian? If you live in a small town, Hopper, you can bet your dating faux pas will come back to haunt you.

Waldon describes herself as 'a comedic actress who can kick ass' and while she considers acting her first love, her extensive work as a stunt performer/co-ordinator and fight choreographer means Hopper really did choose the wrong girl to mess with.

Growing up in East Texas, she graduated with a BA in Theatre Arts from the University of Houston. She has combined both her fighting and acting skills in two successful and quirky theatre productions. Reinventing classic action movies as comedic stage shows, *Point Break Live!* and *Terminator Too!* feature Waldon as both performer and fight choreographer.

HOMEWORK
Is this quiz making you hate me yet?

1. What do Mike, Dustin and Lucas tell their parents they're up to after school in order to sneak off and look for Will?

2. What code name do the boys use for their plan to find Will?

3. Lucas has brought military binoculars and knife, which conflict do they hail from?

4. What does Officer Callaghan assume Doctor Brenner is building at Hawkins National Laboratory?

5. Nancy has a poster of which Hollywood star in her bedroom?

6. Who is it that spots Jonathan's peeping tom photography and tells Steve?

7. In the world of algebra, or at least algebra-the-Carol-way, what is the solution of ten plus 'y'?

8. What does Mike's mum bring Joyce (other than increased stress levels)?

9. What's the name of Hawkins High School's football team?

10. What insult does Mike use to describe Troy?

ADDITIONAL RESEARCH
Cause a major family argument purely by not explaining yourself properly.

NOTES

THE DNA OF STRANGER THINGS: JOHN CARPENTER

THE MOVIES

From cult beginnings with the comedic sci-fi picture *Dark Star* (1974) and tense siege experience *Assault on Precinct 13* (1976), Carpenter's career really soared when someone bearing a passing resemblance to William Shatner started slicing up babysitters.

Halloween (1978) didn't entirely invent the slasher movie but it certainly created the mould that would be used for decades to follow. Who needs the Gothic or the supernatural when you can terrify cinemagoers with nothing more than a nut job and a weapon?[9] Oh, and talent, yes, you need that too, lots of it, though a number of later filmmakers – including those who worked on later movies in the series – arguably forgot that bit.

From the innovative opening tracking shot on, Carpenter proved that he could not only frame perfect images (those lovely wide frames), he could also play your nerves like

---

9   Quick, random list of outlandish weapons used in slasher movies (and I'm ignoring the weird dream kills in the *Nightmare on Elm Street* movies, though would have included Freddy Krueger's gardening glove with blades attached were it not for the fact that it's become so iconic it seems strangely normal now): shish kebab (*Happy Birthday to Me*, 1981); garden shears (*The Burning*, 1981); sleeping bag (*Friday the 13th Part VII: The New Blood*; 1988); prosthetic hand (*Scream Bloody Murder*, 1972); reindeer horns, ho, ho, ho (*Silent Night, Deadly Night*, 1984). See how many you can add to the list!

guitar strings. The movie grossed seventy million dollars worldwide, led to nine sequels and is ranked as one of the most seminal horror movies of all time. Not bad for an independent picture shot in four weeks with a budget of $300,000. Oh, and as well as giving Carpenter his big break, it launched the career of Jamie Lee Curtis too. Hooray for *Halloween*.

All credit to Carpenter, while all of his movies have a distinctive look and flavour, he wasn't so dull as to retread the same old territory either. From psychos in suburbia he went on to give us zombie pirates in *The Fog* (1980); dystopian action in *Escape from New York* (1981); predatory alien shape-shifters in *The Thing* (1982);[10] a possessed car in Stephen King adaptation, *Christine* (1983); sci-fi romance in *Starman* (1984); comic, kung-fu fantasy in *Big Trouble in Little China* (1986); the devil reborn via glowing, sentient goo in *Prince of Darkness* (1987); 'Rowdy' Roddy Piper, there to kick ass and chew bubblegum (though he's all out of bubblegum) in quirky sci-fi parable *They Live* (1988); an invisible Chevy Chase in *Memoirs of an Invisible Man* (1992);[11] a horror writer whose novels change the world in *In the Mouth of Madness* (1995); creepy space kids in *Village*

---

10   An adaptation of the 1938 novella 'Who Goes There?' by John W. Campbell, Jr. The story was also filmed in 1951 as *The Thing from Another World* and loosely inspired *Horror Express*, one of this author's favourite movies, a 1972 picture in which Peter Cushing and Christopher Lee and a bunch of Cossacks fight an alien on the Trans-Siberian Express.

11   A dream come true for some of his fellow *Saturday Night Live* cast members, allegedly.

of the Damned (1995);[12] Vatican-sponsored vampire hunters in *Vampires* (1998); ghosts on Mars in, yes, you guessed it, *Ghosts Of Mars* (2001) and finally, a haunted asylum in *The Ward* (2010), his last movie to date. The only time he solidly rehashed an idea was in 1996's *Escape from L.A.* A sequel to … well, you don't need me to tell you that, do you?

Many critics claim his talent went off the boil, but I would argue there is much to enjoy in his later movies (most especially *In the Mouth of Madness* which is simply wonderful). Even if he never makes another movie,[13] his insistence – for the most part – on maintaining an independent career, avoiding the studio system and the compromises it would bring, has left us with a string of pure Carpenter and we're lucky to have it.

THE MUSIC

A major part of the atmosphere and tone of Carpenter's movies come from their soundtracks, many of which were composed by Carpenter himself, frequently collaborating

---

12   A remake of Wolf Rilla's 1960 adaptation of the John Wyndham novel *The Midwich Cuckoos*. In a 2011 interview with Vulture.com, Carpenter admitted he wasn't particularly interested in the project, claiming it was "getting rid of a contractual assignment". This is probably why the original movie is better, and the novel far better still.

13   And it seems he has no overriding desire to do so, admitting in a 2015 interview with Billboard.com, "I'm turning 67 this January. Directing is really for the young, to be honest with you. Because it's so hard to do and you have to put up with such shit. So if I have something I'm in love with – I am developing a couple of things, nothing I can talk about right now – but if I love it, I'll do it."

with fellow composer Alan Howarth. Usually simple – and that's a deceptive word, as if it were really simple we'd all be doing it – and synthesiser based, his music functions in the same way as his images. Pulsing, repetitive chords build tension and tone, electronic heartbeats that double down on the tension on screen. It's no wonder that Carpenter's musical contributions to horror and sci-fi have inspired not only filmmakers but musicians in general. His theme to *Halloween*, that fast, repeating piano motif ... the score to *The Fog*, moving from wistful, etheric and ghostly to crunching, pounding, encroaching horror as the fog moves forward, rolling unstoppable through the streets ... Carpenter's music is as beautiful, powerful and recognisable as the films they accompany. It's also terrifying. While Carpenter, in an interview with *The Quietus*, claims: "There are no scary chords – music is only frightening in context. It's not frightening sitting out on its own," I'm going to be cocky enough to disagree, I challenge anyone to listen to the soundtrack to *Prince of Darkness* and not feel a shiver.

In recent years, as his urge to make movies has dwindled, his music career has taken a surprising turn. He signed up with a new music attorney (representing his rights on all his soundtracks) who asked him if he had anything new. As it happened, he and his son Cody had, just for fun, been improvising music. They would play console games for a couple of hours, then head to Carpenter's studio to record, then return to their games. Carpenter also invited his godson Daniel (son of David Davies from The Kinks) to join in, acting as engineer and adding lead guitar on some of the tracks. The music, sixty minutes or so of it, was handed to the attorney. A couple of months later he had a record deal. Sacred Bones, a label specialising in vinyl, wanted to release their work.

The album, eventually called *Lost Themes*, pieces designed to act as triggers for fantasies, movies never shot, was a rich and, above all, very Carpenter chunk of electronica. *Lost Themes II* followed. Then, in an even more surprising turn of events, so did a live tour. Carpenter was open about the fact that the idea was unnerving; speaking to Consequenceofsound.net, he admitted: "I've never played live music on this scale. I'm a little scared. I've just never done it, so I don't know what to expect … There aren't a lot of things that scare John Carpenter, but that is one of them."

The tour, a combination of live versions of his soundtrack cues and material from the *Lost Themes* albums, turned out to be a great success, popular with critics and audiences alike. It seems that Carpenter has found a new way to express his creativity and long may it continue.

"Sometimes," he told *The Quietus*, "we say in America, 'Nobody has a second act.' Well, have fun, man. I'm an old guy and here I am doing this. It's great."

Yes. Yes it is.

THINGS TO MAKE AND DO

Well, after that trawl through episode three and the career of John Carpenter I think we need a couple of dollops of fun, don't we? I know! Let's play dress-up!

YOU TOO CAN BE YOUR FAVOURITE CHARACTERS FROM STRANGER THINGS (WELL, A TINY HANDFUL OF THEM, WE CAN'T BE HERE ALL DAY, I HAVE EPISODE FOUR TO GET ON WITH)

Why should actors have all the fun, eh? We can pretend to be people we're not too. People like …

STEVE

What You Will Need

1. Plenty of hair (or a good wig)
2. Hairspray
3. An optional selection of vintage eighties clothes (absurdly expensive so skip this as you'll already have spent a fortune on the hairspray)

The Look

First, take your hair and put all the hairspray in it, you're looking for lift here, we need all that stuff up top where it can loll like a grape-eating Roman emperor, mid-yawn. Make sure you get a bit of fringe falling back in forehead reaching ecstasy aiming for your left eye. Now, add a polo shirt (white collar), jeans (palest of pale blue) and trainers (Nike, red stripe) and you're good to go.

Activities

But the look is only part of our game, now you need to take your Steve-looking self out into the world and start really Steveing one off. Try these simple activities:

1. Find the bonnet of a car to sit on. Stay there, looking cool.
2. Buy a canned drink and then consume it through a hole in the bottom.[14]
3. Accessorise yourself with a brace of arseholes.
4. Keep making a mess in public places then tidy it up again, looking really contrite.

ELEVEN

What You Will Need
1. A blonde wig.
2. A gross frock.
3. A cardigan.
4. Shamelessness.

The Look
Combine all the above items in the conventional manner and then practise your intense stare in the mirror. As soon as the glass in the mirror cracks you're good to go.

Activities
1. Find your nearest furniture store and spend an hour playing with a recliner chair, occasionally smiling.
2. Go to a fast food burger chain and start eating any leftovers you can find as quickly as possible while nervously looking around.
3. Walk into a supermarket and attempt to steal some frozen waffles. If you're in the UK, Bird's Eye Potato Waffles will

---

14 OF THE CAN.

simply have to do.

4. In order to make the most of your new-found time in prison, pretend you're locked up in there as a test subject for terrible experiments. Convince people of this by frequently staring intently at drinks cans.

JOYCE BYERS

What You Will Need

1. Meryl Streep's hair.
2. Too many cigarettes.
3. Tim Burton's phone number.

The Look

Practice moving around the house really quickly in a state of confusion, talking quickly and losing things.

Activities

1. Go into an electrical shop, find the lighting department. Using your foot to toggle the power switch, set as many lights flashing as you can and then act out a séance, screaming at the security staff as they drag you out.
2. Attempt to convince a shop manager to let you buy all his phones on credit.
3. Attend a funeral, repeatedly shouting, "It's not him!" from the back row.
4. Take out the wall of your house with an axe – or someone else's house if you're confident you can run quickly after all that hard work.

CHAPTER
FOUR

THE BODY

Wwere panning down from the stars again, but this
time we don't find ourselves looking at Hawkins
National Laboratory but the Byers house. At this
stage there's not much to divide them; they're both home to
someone single-mindedly trying to pierce the veil between
our reality and another, darker, place.

The police are trying to tell Joyce that the body of her son
has been found but it's all right, she knows better. Naturally,
nobody believes her, not even her son who is forced to give
in to his youthful hormones and retreat to his bed where he
can listen to Joy Division to really wallow in his happy mood.

Within half an hour he won't be so cynical, and the key to
his change of heart? Nancy of course, a girl he likes so much
he'll forgive her anything.[1] Even interrupting him for a chat
while he's picking out coffins for his dead brother. Nancy's
seen something monstrous too (and no, Officers Powell and
Callaghan, it wasn't a bear) and, like all young men ever, for
Jonathan, her word trumps that of his mother's.

Mike's trust in Eleven is also returned. I moaned a little
in the notes for the last episode about dramatic conflict
created by characters not talking to one another. Here,
Eleven, perhaps the ultimate in uncommunicative characters,
proves her point with a walkie-talkie. It will be a constant
disappointment to me in life that I will never, ever, be able to
win an argument by using a walkie-talkie that communicates

---

1   Except, perhaps, for her taste in men.

with other dimensions.[2]

With both misunderstandings overturned, the action pushes forward. Jonathan and Nancy are developing a photograph of the creature that took Barbara while Mike, Dustin and Lucas dress Eleven up and make tracks for a bigger radio.

All the while, of course, Hawkins's Most Unreliable Lover is proving that he can investigate more than parochial, small-town mishaps. Hopper is coming alive with each new episode, clearly energised by the fact that he has something real to sink his teeth into. It can only be a matter of time, we fear, before he ends up dead in a ditch, a government-issue bullet lodged in his head.

The moment none of us can resist a cheer is, of course, the deep public humiliation of a teenage boy in front of his peers. Which, when you put it like that, makes us all sound awful. Still, movies involving school kid outsiders, bully-bait walking, often include that delicious moment when the bully themselves is publicly savaged. Who hasn't watched the *Back to the Future* movies, eager to see Biff brought down so George can rise up? Who isn't moved by the final stand-off between flaky Teddy and Kiefer Sutherland's sneering Ace Merrill in *Stand By Me*? Whose heart isn't warmed when loveable Carrie White, smeared in pig's blood, electrocutes the high-school principal and burns her classmates to a screaming crisp?

OK, maybe that last one divides people. Still, it's a vital

---

2   Luckily I still have this old mobile phone that I claim can communicate with dead people. "See? Even Abraham Lincoln says it's your turn to do the recycling!"

part of many school-set narratives and it always resonates because most of us have been bullied in our time. We remember how that feels, we remember the shame and the horror of it. When Troy and James bully Mike, Dustin and Lucas it makes us like our heroes even more because we empathise. So when the tables are turned how can we fail to take pleasure in it? Chances are, our bullies, the bullies that prey in the real world, got away with their torture. Schoolyard justice will always reign more in fantasy than it does in real life. But there's some small relief: we can take vicarious pleasure in someone else's victory. Parents claim the best way to deal with bullies is to tell your teacher. No. The best way is to use telekinesis to wring the contents of their bladders out for all to see.

This time the episode is written by Justin Doble (who will return to script the seventh episode). Doble is a co-producer on the show and previously worked with J.J. Abrams and his production company Bad Robot. Doble worked as a script co-ordinator on Abrams's TV series *Fringe*[3] and co-wrote fourth season episode 'Wallflower' as well as a comic based on the show. He also wrote an episode of the short-lived *Almost Human*, also from Bad Robot, and an episode of AMC's feudal, martial-arts show *Into the Badlands*.

---

3   You've seen that, right? Please tell me you've seen that or we'll have a falling out.

FAMILIAR THINGS

Having had a relatively light episode for specific references, here the show flings them at the screen with cocky abandon; indeed, there's one to be found in the title of the episode itself: 'The Body' was the name of the Stephen King novella later adapted for the screen as *Stand By Me*. However much the name may be appropriate for the episode, there's little doubt it was also chosen as an explicit reference.

Pretty. Good.

While there have been little touches throughout, that nod towards Steven Spielberg's *E.T. The Extra-Terrestrial*,[4] the scene where Mike, Dustin and Lucas dress Eleven up in girl's clothes and a blonde wig is the sort of nod that would crick your neck. In the movie, Elliot and his older brother dress their new-found alien friend up so that they can walk the streets with him.

Thanks For Ruining The Game, Asshole

Let's talk about Dan O'Bannon, shall we? Because the name of State Trooper David O'Bannon is a reference to him.

O'Bannon attended Florissant Valley Junior College in Missouri and then USC's film school, where he met John Carpenter, the two of them collaborating on a student film

---

4   Yes, still tired of typing all that out. I'll probably only have to do it another thrty or forty times.

103

called *Dark Star*. O'Bannon co-wrote the screenplay with Carpenter as well as starring in it. He also edited the movie, using an ancient Moviola.[5] The movie was expanded and released theatrically in 1974, Carpenter's debut as a director.

Initially O'Bannon worked in special effects and was attached to Alejandro Jodorowsky's planned adaptation of Frank Herbert's sci-fi novel *Dune*. When the production was cancelled, O'Bannon was left broke and homeless. He moved in with his friend Ronald Shusett and they wrote the story that would eventually become *Alien* (1979), the movie that was to really kickstart O'Bannon's career. Shusett and O'Bannon also co-wrote the screenplay to the wonderful 1981 horror picture *Dead and Buried* and the screenplay that – with quite a bit of tinkering – became 1990's Arnold Schwarzenegger-starring *Total Recall* (based on 'We Can Remember It for You Wholesale', a short story by Philip K. Dick).

Working with Don Jakoby, O'Bannon also scripted helicopter-cop movie *Blue Thunder* as well as both space vampire schlock *Lifeforce* and '50s B-movie homage *Invaders from Mars*, both directed by Tobe Hooper.

He wrote *and* directed *The Return of the Living Dead*, the positively effervescent romp that introduced the idea that zombies eat brains (as opposed to simply whatever they can nibble) so if you've ever staggered around the house, arms held out stiffly in front of you, drawling, "Braaaiiinnnnsss," then it's entirely O'Bannon's fault.

---

5   A Moviola was an editing device that allowed the editor to watch the movie at the same time as editing. It was invented in 1924 (although the model O'Bannon used hailed from 1940).

Please say it's not just me.

O'Bannon died in 2009 but left a career of wonderful work behind him.

From O'Bannon To Bannerman[6]

The Indiana State Trooper guarding the morgue at the coroner's office is reading the novel *Cujo* by Stephen King. *Cujo* is a perfect example of how King can wring great writing from the unlikeliest of ideas. It's about a rabid St Bernard and it's a shame that the author barely remembers writing it. It was completed during a time when King was at the height of his alcoholism. Most people can barely read a great book while drunk, let alone write one.

STRANGER SOUNDS

We open with the song 'Atmosphere' from the ironically named Joy Division.[7] A UK band formed in the late seventies, Joy Division only recorded two albums before the suicide of their singer and lyricist, Ian Curtis. Deciding to rename themselves New Order, they're still recording today. Jonathan is not the only angst-ridden young man to have

---

6   George Bannerman was the Sheriff of the fictional town of Castle Rock, Maine. He featured in three Stephen King stories: *The Dead Zone*, 'The Body' and *Cujo*.

7   The name comes from the novella 'House of Dolls' written by Yehiel De-Nur (under the pen name Ka-Tsetnik 135633), concerning cells of female prisoners in Nazi prison-of-war camps, kept for the sexual gratification of their captors. De-Nur had been an inmate of Auschwitz.

listened to their music on headphones and cried.

We have an encore appearance of The Clash's 'Should I Stay or Should I Go' of course, both from Will singing it via Eleven's souped-up walkie-talkie and when Joyce plays it in the house in an attempt to communicate with him.

While Hopper lies to O'Bannon over drinks, we hear 'Color Dreams' by The Deep, a sixties psychedelic rock band who only released a single album, *Psychedelic Moods: A Mind-Expanding Phenomena*. The album was recorded in four days and the band slept in the studio because they couldn't afford a hotel room. Sadly it wasn't very successful.

HONOURABLE STRANGERS

Here we have the opportunity to kill two birds with one stone because the-coroner-who-completely-doesn't-perform-an-autopsy-on-the-thing-that-isn't-even-a-little-bit-Will-Byers[8] is played by director and executive producer, Shawn Levy.

Levy is a Canadian director, producer and actor. As already discussed, his company 21 Laps produced *Stranger Things* so it's no surprise to see him giving the Duffer Brothers a directorial break.

As a director he's mainly worked in comedy, including 2002's *Big Fat Liar* and the Steve Martin vehicles *Cheaper by the Dozen* (2003) its sequel (2005) and the remake of *The*

---

8   Shortened to 'Morgue Worker' in the credits for some stupid reason.

Pink Panther (2006).[9] He also directed all three *Night at the Museum* movies and 2011's sci-fi action movie *Real Steel.*[10] He is, of course, most famous[11] as Jim in 1986's *Zombie Nightmare*, a film about a teenage hit and run victim who is brought back to life by a voodoo priestess in order to exact his revenge.

---

9   Let's be honest, terribly ill-advised.

10 Based on a short story by Richard Matheson, who I KEEP mentioning, don't I? The story was adapted by Matheson himself into an episode of *The Twilight Zone*. Which I also keep mentioning.

11 In my house only.

HOMEWORK

1. Who normally performs autopsies for Roane County?

2. What's the name of the man who travels into the Upside Down via the winch?

3. While Nancy sits in class, her mind on Barb, the teacher is reading from a famous novella. What is it?

4. What's the name of the grief counsellor, introduced to the pupils of Hawkins Middle School during the assembly held in honour of Will's 'death'?

5. What's the name of the bar where Hopper meets O'Bannon?

6. What does the word odontalgia mean?

7. Who owns the quarry Will's body absolutely was not found in?

8. What's the name of the receptionist at the coroner's office?

9. And what excuse does Hopper give her for returning?

10. Who's a 'nasty mutt'?

ADDITIONAL RESEARCH
1. Watch *Zombie Nightmare* (1986) starring Shawn Levy.
2. Hate me a little bit.

NOTES

THE DNA OF STRANGER THINGS: DAVID CRONENBERG

Canadian master of the New Flesh, David Cronenberg has, in recent years, moved away from his more obvious horror roots. While recent movies such as *Maps to the Stars* (2014) and *Cosmopolis* (2012) have retained a sizeable sense of the grotesque, they're a mile away from the juicy, perverse and chilling sci-fi horrors with which the director made his name.[12]

Cronenberg's cinema has often looked to the terrible, violent potential of scientific study. In the seventies, he was all about medical experiments going awry. In *Shivers* (1975), his first full-length feature, lab-developed, parasitic creatures infect the residents of an apartment block causing the hosts to go on a sexual rampage. *Rabid* followed in 1977, with yet more communicable horror troubling Canada, this time in the form of a vampiric virus that sees the sufferer develop a phallic organ in their armpit that feeds on blood. I should add that, in anyone else's hands, these two pictures would have been schlocky – if possibly fun – trash. One of Cronenberg's gifts is to turn one-line synopses like these into movies that are far cleverer, far more cerebral, than one might think.

After a sidestep into psychology – an area that would come to consume much of his later work – with 1979's *The*

---

12   And so they should be, if an artist – and Cronenberg certainly is one – doesn't progress and diversify what's the point? *Maps to the Stars* may actually be may favourite Cronenberg movie. Sacrilege to some, but you've read enough of this book by now to know I'm used to having my taste questioned.

Brood, 1981's *Scanners* moved into the world of telepathy/ telekinesis. Scanners are people with enhanced mental gifts. Harvested by the movie's villainous ConSec (a weapons manufacturer) they're put to evil use. Infamous (and rightly lauded) for a scene in which a Scanner assassin kills someone by making their head explode, the movie unquestionably leaves its bloodstained fingerprints on *Stranger Things*.

Videodrome (1983) saw Cronenberg really let rip with his obsessions. James Woods, the CEO of a television station, stumbles upon a video of extreme sexual violence. Watching the video alters you, the signal embedded in it causing surreal hallucinations that worsen as time goes on. It is often said that horror is at its best when the grotesque and horrific is merely hinted at, the truly terrible happening off screen or in the shadows. Not here. Still, as Cronenberg himself later joked, it would be difficult to simply imply that James Woods has grown a vagina in his chest, a vagina he then inserts a VHS cassette into. Riffing on the old argument as to whether watching violent imagery can cause the desire to commit violence, *Videodrome* is a cinematic experience like … well, I was going to say 'like no other' but that would be doing a disservice to rest of Cronenberg's work.

The same year saw Cronenberg adapt Stephen King's *The Dead Zone*, with Christopher Walken as Johnny Smith, a schoolteacher who, after a car accident, finds he's developed psychic powers. The movie culminates in Smith discovering that Greg Stillson, a presidential candidate who rides to success on a populist platform of social change, will ultimately kill us all by ordering nuclear strike. If someone could introduce Christopher Walken to Donald Trump that would be lovely. Just in case.

The year 1986 brought further Science Done Bad in *The Fly*, Cronenberg's remake of a fifties movie of the same name. Jeff Goldblum invents a teleportation device that would have worked brilliantly had a fly not accidentally shared his journey, its DNA combining with his. A masterpiece of grisly, icky, horror cinema, it's unquestionably one of his most mainstream pictures. You haven't lived until you've seen a gooey, spine-covered Jeff Goldblum eat a doughnut by throwing up on it first.

After the huge commercial success of *The Fly*, Cronenberg retreated into increasingly personal and less easily defined (though no less accomplished and powerful) movies, including: 1988's *Dead Ringers*, with Jeremy Irons in a dual role as troubled gynaecologist twins; 1991's *Naked Lunch*, an adaption of William Burroughs's not-quite-as-unadaptable-as-you-might-have-thought book and 1996's controversial *Crash*, another novel adaptation, this time J. G. Ballard's novel about people who take sexual pleasure from car crashes.

Always contentious, cerebral, challenging and powerful, David Cronenberg is one of our most important moviemakers. If you're unfamiliar with his work you owe it to yourself to remedy the fact, however daunting or difficult some of it may appear.

NOTES

CHAPTER
FIVE

THE FLEA AND THE ACROBAT

H

opper just doesn't care, does he? Strolling through the corridors of Hawkins National Laboratory, unzipping radiation warnings, fighting guards. He's a man on a mission, and with every step we're composing possible eulogies for him.[1] He means to find Will Byers, whatever it takes. Turns out what it'll take is four more episodes but then, anyone who has seen anything, ever, knew that. Still, it could have been worse: at least they won't be four episodes without Hopper, which, considering what happened to Benny back in the first episode, is something of a relief. A surprise too. I suppose it's slightly trickier to assassinate police chiefs than cooks.

Meanwhile, Lonnie Byers is pouring Joyce a drink to 'help her think straight'. Lonnie has got drinking all wrong. But that's OK, because he's got some reassuring words: "I think you need to seriously consider the possibility that all this is in your head. Remember your Aunt Darlene." We never do get to hear what madness Darlene wrought upon the world but that's OK, because it can't be as mad as Lonnie himself; he doesn't approve of *The Evil Dead* so screw him. Naturally he's only returned to the family in the hope of cashing in on his son's death. We can but hope he's later involved in an attempt to feign a road accident in order to claim the insurance and that it goes horribly wrong.

Still, by the end of the episode Joyce is in a much better position than where she started, Hopper believes her and plans are about to be hatched.

---

1   "Jim Hopper, you never called back but at least you paid the bill."

Jonathan's plan is to shoot things. Sadly it's not his forte, nor is chatting up Nancy, though it's a lovely moment where he clearly colours his view of her with his own preconceived notions. All power to this episode's writer, Alison Tatlock. She knows how heads work, unsurprising given her experience writing scripts for HBO's *In Treatment*. It's a lovely moment for Nancy, more empowering and clever than her ability to kill empty beer cans. It's a slight shame she finishes the episode by throwing such wit and wisdom away. Nancy, dear, you're not an idiot but only idiots crawl into gooey, Magic Hell Trees.

And what about the Loser's Club? Well, they're being Wil Wheaton, River Phoenix, Cory Feldman and Jerry O'Connell this week. The school principal considers them 'less athletic types' but look at them go! Hiking! Wrestling! Oh … Cynical Lucas rears his head again and it seems our sense of camaraderie is taking a beating already, as are Lucas's ribs. That'll teach him to pick a fight with Eleven's boyfriend; science is neat but not very forgiving.

FAMILIAR THINGS

Two visual references this episode. Firstly, the spirit of Rob Reiner's *Stand By Me* is directly evoked with the shot of Mike, Dustin, Lucas and Eleven walking along the train tracks. As mentioned elsewhere,[2] *Stand By Me* was a touchstone for the Duffer Brothers and, back in the

---

2   Possibly ad nauseam.

director's chair (where they'll stay for the rest of the run) there's no doubt the image was offered quite intentionally.

The other familiar visual element in this episode is the featureless black space Eleven finds herself in when astral travelling. It's awfully similar to the weird 'elsewhere' Scarlett Johansson lures men to in 2013's *Under the Skin*.

STRANGER SOUNDS From Joy Division to their next incarnation, New Order. We hear their 1985 piece 'Elegia', a waltz of synth and crunchy guitars, during Will's 'funeral'.

Originally a seventeen-minute composition, written in memory of Ian Curtis,[3] the version included on their album *Low-Life* was cut-down to just under five minutes. For a few years, a poor-quality copy of the full-length version could be found online but it was officially released in 2002 as part of a CD box set, then again in 2008 on the reissue of the *Low-Life* album.

While Hopper indulges in a spot of paranoid home improvement we hear 'Green Desert' by Tangerine Dream. The title track from their 1986 album, it was actually recorded in 1973.

The final track we hear is 'Nocturnal Me' from UK rock band Echo & the Bunnymen. The song comes from their 1984 album *Ocean Rain*.

---

3   See the Stranger Sounds section for the previous episode.

HONOURABLE STRANGERS

Well, I suppose we ought to finally single out Ross Partridge, who plays Lonnie. After all, excluding an actor because of the horrible character he plays is rather like telling off your sandwich after it's made you feel full.

Partridge attended the University of California in Santa Cruz. He'd initially had no interest in acting – his goal had been to study film with a view to making them one day – but his room-mate convinced him to audition for the theatrical version of *12 Angry Men* and he loved the experience.[4] He worked in a lot of theatre – with small TV roles to help pay the bills – before building a CV of appearances in indie films such as 2011's *The Off Hours* and 2013's *Mutual Friends*. In 2014 he wrote, directed and starred in the movie *Lamb*, based on the novel by Bonnie Nadzam.

---

4   Originally a television play by Reginald Rose, broadcast in 1954, it was adapted the following year for the stage and then, most famously, turned into a movie starring Henry Fonda in 1957.

HOMEWORK

1. There's a stuffed toy on Eleven's bed at the Hawkins National Laboratory, what is it?

2. A girl is crying at Will's funeral and Dustin can't wait to tell Will. What's her name?

3. What colour are the fireballs Will is drawing in the flashback during this episode?

4. Where does Hopper find a listening device in his home?

5. When broaching the subject of alternate dimensions with Mr Clarke, Mike cites a TV series/book and the author behind both. Name them.

6. Whose 'Many Worlds Interpretation' does Mr Clarke assume the boys have been thinking about?

7. Name the two hunters who have gone missing near Mirkwood.

8. What movie does Steve offer to take Nancy to see?

9. How many cans does Jonathan manage to hit when practising with the revolver?

10. How old was Steve when his dad forced him to kill a rabbit?

NOTES

THE DNA OF STRANGER THINGS – ELECTRONIC MEDITATION

As previously admitted, it's not just the look of *Stranger Things* that owes a debt to other things, it's the music too. While I've discussed the songs used in the show – and bowed before the majesty of its original soundtrack – we should take a moment to point out some of the musicians who, in one way or another, informed it.[5]

Now, as I did when discussing the references touched on by the Duffer Brothers, let me make a caveat here: Dixon and Stein's music stands thoroughly on its own two feet; it's no more a wholesale regurgitation of other people's work than the show it accompanies. There's a lazy trend in pointing to an electronic score and immediately accusing it of being a piece of nostalgia. As if you would point to someone playing an electric guitar and, regardless of the music they were playing, state, "You're just rehashing Jimi Hendrix, because he also played a guitar." Yes, there are times when the soundtrack evokes the sound of other musicians but, for its vast majority it is resolutely the work of the two, terribly talented, musicians who created it.

Though of course, every creative is influenced by their loves, so, for this section I have intentionally chosen the three artists mentioned by Dixon and Stein as being influences on their sound in an interview with *Rolling Stone*.

---

5   If you're dipping in and out, John Carpenter is discussed elsewhere so don't tear the book up in fury.

So, let's pop on our headphones and relive electronica gone by.

TANGERINE DREAM

Tangerine Dream are a German group founded in 1967 by Edgar Froese. Over the years their membership has constantly evolved, with musicians joining and leaving regularly, though Froese was a fixed point up until his death in 2015.

Their output is frankly staggering, 103 albums (including studio albums and live recordings, which often contained original material) and thirty-four soundtracks (mostly movies but they composed music for *Grand Theft Auto V* too). This doesn't include the many – oh so many – compilations of their work over the years.

The band moved from psychedelic rock beginnings to the more electronic based sound the band is known for. Part of this change came through Christopher Franke who joined the band in 1970.[6]

Franke was initially a drummer but also an early adaptor of analogue sequencers – an electronic device used to record and loop music – and one of the first musicians to use them as part of a live performance. Together, Froese and Franke embraced synthesisers and keyboards, and Tangerine Dream as we know it was established. Franke stayed with

---

6   Sci-fi fans will no doubt be familiar with Franke's name thanks to his composing the soundtrack to TV show *Babylon 5* for its five-year run.

Tangerine Dream for seventeen years.

With an ever-shifting sound, moving through various styles of electronica, from krautrock, to new-age to influencing the sound of dance music, Tangerine Dream are an electronic legend.

Perhaps inevitably though, most people are familiar with them thanks to their extensive work providing movie soundtracks, some of their most famous being *Sorcerer* (1977), *Thief* (1981), *Risky Business* (1983),[7] *Firestarter* (1984) *Legend* (1985) and *Near Dark* (1987).

GOBLIN

Italian band Goblin are also predominantly known for their soundtrack work and have something of a confusing membership, though the core members are certainly Claudio Simonetti (keyboards), Massimo Morante (guitar) and Fabio Pignatelli (bass).

Originally known as Oliver, then – once signed to a record label – Cherry Five, Goblin's debut release (also called *Cherry Five*) impressed film director Dario Argento so much that he signed them up to work alongside composer Giorgio Gaslini to compose a soundtrack to his film *Profondo Rosso*.[8] When Gaslini left, after a disagreement with Argento, on the third of four recording days, the band were given the

---

7   Yes, featuring Steve's OTHER rival for Nancy's affections.

8   Released in the UK and US as *Deep Red* and mentioned in the 'Familiar Things' section for the second episode.

opportunity to create an entirely new soundtrack. As long as they could still deliver on time. Meaning they had less than forty-eight hours to compose and record.

This daunting proposition was the making of them. Their soundtrack was a huge success – and rightly so, it's phenomenal – and was a huge chart success in Italy.

The success brought a second album, *Roller*, in 1976, the soundtrack to Argento's next film *Suspiria* (1977) and a couple of other soundtrack commissions, culminating in their music for George A. Romero's *Dawn of the Dead* (1978).

At which point it all becomes a bit fragmented and confusing as the band fell out. A partial reunion occurred – with Simonetti, Pignatelli and Morante being credited individually by name rather than as Goblin – for Argento's 1982 movie *Tenebrae*, and again for his 1985 movie *Phenomena* (though Morante was missing). All three were back in 2000 for Argento's *Non Ho Sonno* but the reunion was short-lived. These days, reunions – predominantly for live shows – appear under a confusing mess of names (Claudio Simonetti's Goblin, Back to the Goblin, Goblin Rebirth etc.) each spearheaded by one or, very occasionally, two of the trio but never including all three.

On his own, Simonetti provided a number of further movie soundtracks for Argento: *Demoni* (1985), *Opera* (1987), *Il cartaio* (2004), *La terza madre* (2007) and *Dracula 3D* (2012).

GIORGIO MORODER

Giorgio Moroder is an Italian singer, composer and producer and pop music would be a poorer place without him. He's worked with artists as diverse as David Bowie, Kylie Minogue and Blondie (with whom he co-wrote the classic 'Call Me').

He started his career in 1963, as a singer/songwriter but really hit his stride in the seventies, working with Donna Summer. His bright, energetic, electronic sound crept into countless acts in the eighties, as disco as a glitterball, and he even compiled a – somewhat controversial – new cut of Fritz Lang's 1927 silent cinema classic, *Metropolis*.

As a soundtrack composer, his most well-known work – and singled out for attention by Michael Stein – is probably the score he composed alongside Harold Faltermeyer for 1986's *Top Gun*. The lead song from which, 'Take My Breath Away', recorded by Berlin won both an Academy Award and a Golden Globe and is the work Moroder is most proud of.[9]

Outside of *Top Gun* he also racked up a daunting list of other soundtracks, including *Midnight Express* (1978), *Cat People* (1982), *Flashdance* (1983), *Scarface* (1983) and *The NeverEnding Story* (1984).

Now in his seventies, he still works as a DJ and producer and was featured on Daft Punk's 2013 album *Random Access Memories*, an album of music calling back to an eighties disco sound.

---

9   According to a 2015 interview with the Australian Broadcasting Corporation.

NOTES

HOMEWORK

Listen to the soundtrack to *Suspiria* by Goblin
(and never sleep soundly again).

NOTES

CHAPTER SIX

THE MONSTER

"All three of you were being a bunch of little assholes, I was the only reasonable one."

Dustin, how I love you. He's got a point too, the 'love triangle' of Mike, Eleven and Lucas has come to a head and it's going to take a little while (say an episode or so) before things can be resolved. Dustin, king of compasses and group therapist will keep us happy in the meantime. Ah … that look when Mike insists Dustin's his best friend as well as Lucas … adorable.

There are sweet moments between Nancy and Jonathan too. Nothing brings a boy and girl together quite like shopping for weaponry. Even being arrested for punching Steve repeatedly in the face only serves to bring out Nancy's caring nature. Oh Duffer Brothers, we just know where you're going with this! Of course Jonathan and Nancy are going to end up together!

And then there's Hopper and Joyce, Hawkins's small town version of *Scarecrow and Mrs King*.[1] They've met Eleven's mother! Probably.

I also note with something approaching mortal fear how many people online have considered it necessary to point out that Hopper uses a weird device in this episode: a callbox. Thank you Internet, yes I suppose I am quite old if I consider callboxes perfectly normal. Yes, I remember when the

---

1   US TV series that started in 1983, running for four seasons. It involved the divorced mother of two boys (Kate Jackson) becoming involved with a secret service agent (Bruce Boxleitner) and getting involved in lots of jolly scrapes. And, no, I'm not suggesting it's a reference, not remotely.

Internet you love so much wasn't even a thing. Or omnipresent mobile phones. Oh God … I was going to type DVD and Blu-ray then realised that:

a) They're old-fashioned already, and …

b) I'm actually old enough to remember the point at which VHS tapes became something you could afford to buy rather than just rent.

Well, this section has just become depressing … YES I WAS ONLY A FEW YEARS YOUNGER THAN MIKE IN 1983 STOP GOING ON ABOUT IT.[2]

Where was I? Oh yes … Noting how – with the exception of Mike and Lucas – this episode features multiple moments of bonding between the characters. Perhaps the ultimate example being Eleven's grandstanding reappearance at the climax, saving Mike's life, which culminates in the lovely three-way hug between her, Mike and Dustin. There's even the hope of Lucas Rambo returning to the fold, as he watches the forces of 'Hawkins Power and Light' mobilise in pursuit of his friends.

Naturally, given we're motoring towards the climax of our story, we can't be sure how long these relationships will last. We're old hands in the story mines, we know the rules, there's chaos to come and who knows who will still be standing by the time the dust settles?

The script for this episode was written by Jessie Nickson-Lopez, staff writer on the show.[3]

---

2   I may have gone for a little lie down and a cry at this point.

3   The role of a staff writer can vary from show to show but in general it's someone who works in the writing room, an extra creative muscle that can help with brainstorming ideas, discussing plot points and generally bolstering the writing talent.

FAMILIAR THINGS

A bit thin on the ground again this time, though we do get a very nice picture of a shark while Nancy's discussing the possible hunting methods of the creature from the Upside Down.

If the Duffer Brothers don't mean to channel the spirit of John Rambo then Lucas certainly does as he prepares for battle, most especially in the headband. Whatever happens out there, at least Lucas knows his forehead can blend in with the trees. Certainly Lucas, with all his ex-Nam gear, must have loved *First Blood* (1982), the movie that launched the Rambo franchise.

The final scene with Troy threatening Dustin with a knife is pure *It*. In Stephen King's novel, bully Henry Bowers threatens the portly Ben Hanscom, cutting his belly with a knife. Ben doesn't have the advantage of a telekinetic friend to help save the day.

STRANGER SOUNDS

We go song crazy this week.

Corey Hart's 'Sunglasses at Night' accompanies Steve, Terry and Carol as they drive over to Nancy's house. Canadian Corey has one of the biggest, most alarming mouths in eighties pop – or maybe it just seems that way because he's miming in the promo video for this song, a terrifying tale of secret police demanding Hart wears his shades. The song was taken from his honestly-titled debut album *First Offence*. The album was recorded in the UK, at the Revolution Recording Studios in Manchester. Allegedly the inspiration for the lyric came from the fact that they took to wearing sunglasses in the control room because a badly positioned air conditioning unit kept blowing in their faces. So, it could easily have been called 'Cory Asked Them to Turn the AC Down a Bit' or 'Tell the Canadian Ponce to Bugger Off to London if 'E Can't Take a Bit of Breeze'.

Mr Clarke is a classy chap, as he not only proves with that moustache but also by listening to Bach. To be precise: the first movement of his Violin Concerto in E major, BWV 1042. As Douglas Adams once said: "Beethoven tells you what it's like to be Beethoven and Mozart tells you what it's like to be human. Bach tells you what it's like to be the universe."

Then, when Karen Wheeler proves she's the coolest – and yet most terrifying – mum ever by swiftly and painlessly picking Nancy's door lock with a hairpin,[4] we hear 'I See the Future' by Andrew Pinching which is actually a track produced for commercial use in TV and film rather than being a pop song of the time. Andrew Pinching (also known as Pinch) is the drummer for punk band The Damned, having joined in 1999.

While Nancy and Jonathan go shopping for things to hunt monsters with, we hear from those giants of country music, Dolly Parton. She's singing 'The Bargain Store', one of her most famous songs, not least because a misunderstanding over one of the lyrics ("You can easily afford the price")

---

4   Not, as my auto-correct would try to have me believe, a 'harpoon', though it's a scene I would love to see.

led some radio stations to believe the song was about prostitution so refused to play it.

We have a return visit from Tangerine Dream during Steve and Jonathan's fight, with the track 'Exit' from their 1981 album of the same name. As a pleasing little side-note, the final track on the album is named after Eleven's enforced hobby during her time in captivity: 'Remote Viewing'.

HONOURABLE STRANGERS

Aimee Mullins, who plays the unfortunate Terry Ives, is, well, just a bit amazing frankly. Born with fibula hemimelia (the absence of fibula bones) she had both legs amputated below the knee. She became a keen sportsperson at school, playing softball and skiing.[5] She was the first athlete to use the Flex-Foot Cheetah, carbon-fibre prosthetics, and competed in various field and track events as well as taking part in the 1996 Paralympics.

She retired from competitive sports in 1998, launching a new career as a fashion model the following year. She worked extensively with Alexander McQueen and was appointed a global ambassador for L'Oréal in 2011.

She is also well known for her speaking appearances, notably as part of the TED conference.

Oh, and she's an actor too; you may have spotted that because here she is, doing it terribly well. Appearances

---

5   Not at the same time, even Aimee Mullins isn't that amazing.

include Oliver Stone's *World Trade Centre*, an episode of ITV's *Poirot*[6] and the John-Malkovich-is-a-pirate series *Crossbones* in 2014.

---

6   The adaptation of *Five Little Pigs* in 2003.

HOMEWORK

1. What's the name of the club that Connie 'I Killed Benny' Frazier most definitely isn't setting up, whatever she tells Mr Clarke?

2. What happened on the Bloodstone path?

3. While shopping for waffles, Eleven calls a supermarket employee a mouth breather. What's his name?

4. How many boxes does she steal?

5. Based on the books next to her, Terry Ives is - or at least was - keen on what horticultural hobby?

6. When did Dustin arrive at Hawkins Middle School?

7. When does Becky think her sister miscarried?

8. Hawkins Hunting and Camping store is having a sale on army surplus stock! Good news for monster hunters everywhere. What discount are they offering?

9. What's the name of the movie theatre in Hawkins?

10. What does Tommy graffiti in the alley?

ADDITIONAL RESEARCH

Figure out something that was commonplace in your youth but is now utterly obsolete. Then weep.

NOTES

THE DNA OF STRANGER THINGS – THE TRUTH IS OUT THERE

Bearing in mind these are big subjects, subjects that have had shelves full of books dedicated entirely to each (see the Homework section), I can only give you the most basic of mission briefings. Nonetheless, shove your night-vision goggles in a bag, pull your smartest balaclava into place and let's clip our way through the electrified wire fence of secret government projects.

A BORING NOTE ON TRUTH

I will assume you understand that while I will relate the stories as if they were genuine – because that's just nicer – most of the 'facts' about the first two projects discussed here are contested.[7] For every conspiracy theorist that presents these stories as genuine, there are just as many people – often many more – who consider them nonsense and even offer to disprove them. Naturally, this bothers the conspiracy theorist not one jot because, "Well, they would try to do that, wouldn't they?" Which is true, I suppose. "They" would.

Still, we're living in an age where truth is a more

---

7   Preston B. Nichols and Peter Moon – the prime originators of the stories about the Montauk Project – have the most wonderful expression in their book *The Montauk Project: Experiments in Time*. "Some of the data you will read in this book can be considered as 'soft facts'. Soft facts are not untrue, they are just not backed up by irrefutable documentation." In other words, apparently, they can't prove a word of it.

complicated thing than ever and while I certainly don't dismiss conspiracy theories out of hand, I also consider it important that 'don't believe everything you're told' works both ways. There is a comfort, an excitement, in siding with the conspiracy theorist because most of us naturally distrust the claims of authority (unless you're Ted Wheeler of course). The conspiracy theorist has all the best stories. Their claims are exciting and, often, we'd prefer to believe them because they would make our world a more interesting place. However, sometimes an exhaust trail from an airplane is just an exhaust trail, yes?

Many conspiracies are no more than enthusiastic fiction dressed up in the smart clothes of truth. Some may be true, some clearly, *obviously* aren't and it's the opinion of this author that spreading badly researched theories – yes, Facebook memes, I'm looking at you – and classing them as fact is no less pernicious than any lie those in power may tell you. Believe nobody until you've tried to disprove them and failed.

But enough of this, let us throw our scepticism to the winds – where a secret government stealth fighter built using salvaged UFO parts can blast it to shreds – and simply immerse ourselves in the possibilities.

THE PHILADELPHIA EXPERIMENT

October, 1943, the Philadelphia Naval Shipyard in Pennsylvania. The US military are sponsoring what they call the Rainbow Project, an experiment that – if successful

– could help them win the war. They hope to be able to make a ship entirely invisible to radar. By altering the electromagnetic field surrounding an object, it is thought radar waves will be diverted around it. The scientists of the Rainbow Project have been using the USS *Eldridge* as their test vessel. Early tests have seen some limited success, with the ship becoming partly invisible. The crew haven't enjoyed the experience much though, experiencing, at best, nausea, at worst, becoming imbedded within the steel fabric of the ship itself. Never fun.

One final experiment – held on 28th October – saw the ship vanish entirely, reappearing two hundred miles away in Norfolk, Virginia where it was seen by the crew of the SS *Andrew Furuseth*. The *Eldridge* then vanished again, reappearing back in Philadelphia where it started. It later transpired that not only had the ship moved in space, it had also moved approximately ten minutes back in time.

The crew were severely traumatised – those who weren't hanging out of the bulkheads having become one with the fabric of the ship – and the experiments were halted.

THE MONTAUK PROJECT

After the failure of Project Rainbow – or success, depending on how you look at it – a number of the researchers involved wished to continue their work. The US Congress rejected the idea as far too dangerous. Not to be deterred, those researchers petitioned the Department of Defense, claiming their work could develop a weapon that would drive an enemy insane. The Department of Defense agreed, without congressional approval, and set up the Phoenix Project, a top-secret base in Long Island. Initial funding was provided by ten billion dollars of Nazi gold that had been discovered in France.

Initially the base was set up at the Brookhaven National Laboratory (sound familiar?) but then, when researchers realised they would need a larger satellite dish, was moved to a nearby decommissioned US Air Force base, in Montauk.

Work progressed under the stewardship of Nikola Tesla (no, he didn't actually die in 1943, that was a cunning cover-up, the 86-year-old genius was simply squirrelled away to become Director of Operations of the Phoenix Project).

Work covered many areas, from teleportation to constructing flying saucers, faking the moon landing to creating the AIDS virus. They developed mind control methods, contacted alien life and even bio-engineered monstrous creatures and/or humans with enhanced abilities. It was, in short, your one-stop shop for every secret government project you ever heard of. If it wasn't for the work of the Phoenix Project, the X-Files would have had to finish after its first season.

Then, in 1983, the time-travel division made contact with the USS *Eldridge* of 1943 providing a wonderfully neat, circular shape to our story. Sadly, a by-product of the time tunnel created between the two time zones saw the USS *Eldridge* sent into hyperspace, where it became trapped until staff from the future managed to disrupt the 1943 experiment and return the ship to its correct place in time.

Shortly after this either the project was shut down – with

all involved either brainwashed, shot or sworn to secrecy –
OR work continues to this day, with even tighter security.[8]

What's that? The area where the Air Force base used to
be is now a National Park, in fact has been ever since 2002?
Don't worry, that was just extra cover, research continues in
underground chambers below the park.

MKULTRA

From the giddy heights of unprovable 'soft facts' we move
to genuine history. Project MKUltra was a wide-ranging
programme of experiments on human subjects conducted by
the CIA. And it absolutely did happen (though entirely *what*
happened under its watch is largely unknown).

The operation was set up in the early fifties (officially
sanctioned in 1953) and was designed to explore areas of
mind control and drug use, with a particular focus on using
the latter to force confessions from enemy agents.

Early experiments focused strongly on the effects of
LSD, and while there were many programmes – such
as the one Terry Ives clearly took part in – that targeted
students in need of an 'easy' payday, the drug was also often
administered to people without their knowledge or consent
(a violation of the Nuremberg Code that the US agreed to
post WWII, but never mind). Subjects would then be studied
to understand the various effects the drug might have.

MKUltra also sought to develop new drugs that could

---

8   I know which I'd choose.

achieve various results. Most were designed as a weapon against enemy agents (drugs that would cause brain damage, lethargy, loss of memory etc.) but also some that might prove beneficial to US operatives, boosting their abilities.

In 1973, as the US government reeled from the Watergate scandal,[9] the project was halted and all files destroyed so we will never know the full extent of the researches conducted during its twenty-odd years of existence. Nor can we prove whether a Dr Martin Brenner was on staff. Still, the project was certainly huge with a grand total of fifty-four colleges/universities, fifteen research foundations/pharmaceutical companies, twelve hospitals and three prisons known to have been involved.

There were certainly some deaths associated with the project, most famously that of Frank Olson, an army biochemist who was given LSD without his knowledge and jumped to his death (or was he pushed?) from the thirteenth floor of a New York city hotel a week later.

---

9   The revelation of a number of illegal activities – such as bugging the headquarters of the Democratic Party – conducted by members of President Nixon's administration.

HOMEWORK

The Montauk Project: Experiments in Time
by Preston B. Nichols and Peter Moon
The first in a series of books published by Sky Books
(publisher slogan: 'Where science fiction meets reality')
that are either sci-fi novels presenting themselves as factual
or, exactly what they appear, non-fiction books exposing
scurrilous shenanigans on Long Island and elsewhere. Sky
Books publish books on a number of popular conspiracy
themes, including The Philadelphia Experiment, many
of them written by Moon. It seems to be either a cottage
industry in truth dissemination or a whopping fiction
franchise. Perhaps it doesn't matter, they're certainly fun
reads.

The Philadelphia Experiment (1984)
The idea of the Philadelphia experiment (and the Montauk
Project) was turned into a movie directed by Stewart Raffill.
It is only loosely based on the conspiracy theories – but as
we can't confirm them what's a little more storytelling fun
matter? Two sailors (played by Michael Paré and Bobby Di
Cicco) find themselves transported off the deck of the USS
Eldridge and transported to 1984 where similar experiments
threaten to destroy the world.

Banshee Chapter (2013)
A low-budget horror picture written and directed by Blair
Erickson that combines elements from H.P. Lovecraft's
story 'From Beyond' with the experiments conducted

during Project MKUltra. It stars Ted Levine who is clearly pretending to be renowned journalist Hunter S. Thompson throughout.[10] Surprisingly creepy and effective, it rises above its low budget and delivers a genuine sense of unease.

THINGS TO MAKE AND DO

Look, the US Government are bound to be on their way, in
a couple of hours' time we're all going to be strapped to a
table, brimming to the back teeth with LSD, awaiting a sound
brainwashing and/or a bullet to the head. So we may as well have
a bit of fun while we wait, yes? Let's have …

FUN WITH LIGHTBULBS

What You Will Need:
1. Twenty-six battery-operated tea lights.
2. A bit of wood that's big enough to attach all the lights to it in three rows (9 x 9 x 8).
3. A marker pen to write on the wood.

Right then, your first problem is attaching the lights to the board. If the switches turning them on and off are on the bottom of the tealights (and of COURSE they are, they ALWAYS are) then you're going to need to drill some big holes. In an ideal world, you would drill/cut holes in the

---

10   Probably most famous for his portrayal of Buffalo "It puts the lotion on its skin" Bill in 1991's *The Silence of the Lambs*.

wood that would allow the tealights to sit neatly in them so that the bulbs stick out on one side while you, hiding around the back like a right silly tinker, have clear finger-flipping access to the switches. Yes, that would be best. Do that.[11] Make sure you leave enough space above each light to be able to write, in nice bold script, a letter of the alphabet. Above each light, in nice bold script, write a letter of the alphabet.

Then, write the letters on the back too, by the switches, so you know what you're doing. I'm not saying you're not clever enough to be able to match the switches on the back with the letters written on the front but, well, you're doing this so you're obviously a *bit* stupid. Just write them on, it's for the best.

You have created the Joyce Byers Sparkling Séance Board! Yay!

Now, Joyce Byers had two distinct advantages over us:
1. She had the good fortune of having a vanished son who could operate Christmas lights entirely by the power of his mind. This was quick, colourful and saved on a lot of switch-flicking.
2. She cared enough to have the patience to wait for answers spelled out in such a tedious fashion; your friends may not

---

11   It's easy doing craft guides when you don't have to build them yourself. If I tried this there would be several hours of swearing and a small clan of cats wondering why their owner was bleeding/crying/banging his head with a large piece of wood.

have this.[12]

Regardless, we press on! This is now your sole method of communication; this is how you speak to the world. When you want to greet someone, get flipping. H.E.L.L.O. you will say, one painful letter at a time. I.L.I.K.E.S.T.R.A.N.G.E.R.T.H. I.N.G.S.D.O.Y.O.U.[13]

"What's wrong with you?" they'll say, all quick and voicey. N.O.T.H.I.N.G. you'll reply, I.V.E.B.U.I.L.T.A.J.O.Y.C.E.B.Y.E. R.S.S.P.A.R.K.L.I.N.G.S.E.A.N.C.E.B.O.A.R.D.D.O.Y.O.U.L.I. K.E.I.T.

(At which point you will look up from your switches to deploy your quizzical eyebrow only to discover that everyone in the world you thought loved you has gone, never to return.)

Initially, this may seem like a bad thing but then you'll realise that means you don't have to flip any more switches so it's a relief all round.

---

12 They won't, they just won't, this is going to be all the annoying and I doubt anyone will want to know you once we're done.

13 We forgot about question marks, didn't we? Never mind. If you're a stickler for grammar then feel free to add one. Either that or practise raising a quizzical eyebrow, a lovely little move you could throw in after the lights.

CHAPTER SEVEN

THE BATHTUB

The bad men are coming … all of them … get out of there!"

I can't be the only one who spent young summers belting along on my bike imagining terrible people were chasing me? Please don't tell me I was just a horribly paranoid child.

Lucas shouts his garbled warning on the walkie-talkie and it's all burning bike rubber and flipped trucks for a few minutes. It was, as Wise Dustin would say, awesome. But let's discuss the elephant in the room. Let's talk about the sad day Karen 'I can pick locks with a hairpin' Wheeler decided to marry the dullest man in the world.

Ted Wheeler is punching well above his weight. Even Nancy knows it.

"This is our government," he tells his wife, "they're on our side." Yes Ted. Of course they are, go and fall asleep in the La-Z-Boy with a plate of chicken. What terrible life did Karen Wheeler need to escape from that a life with a Mogadon in a cardigan seemed a fair trade? To hell with Will, when are we all going to get together and rescue poor Karen? She's trapped in the Never Mind.

Look, Ted! The soft-spoken Mathew Modine, evil gravy poured over every scene, is sat at your kitchen table asking: "Will you trust me?" Surely anyone with a functioning frontal lobe should be thinking, "No, Mr Evil Suit, I really, really, won't." Your wife knows. "That man gives me the creeps," she admits. Yes Karen, of course he does. Now get a divorce.

I am looking at every scene she has with Nancy and imagining the question she never quite asks – but is always thinking – "Just tell me one thing, darling, is this Steve Harrington more interesting than your father? Don't do what I did. Don't marry a beige pair of slacks."

Still, Nancy has more important things to think about. The coming together I talked about during the last episode comes to full fruition here as all our heroes are finally on the same page (and in the same room). We even have Mr Lover-Boy Clarke on the phone. Plans are being hatched and we're ready for one final push to rescue Will and Bar … Oh, maybe not Barb. Oh well, you can't have everything.[1]

What a lovely moment we have with Mike and Nancy. "No more secrets," she insists, "from now on we tell each other everything." They then proceed to lie to one another. Brothers and sisters, it was always so.

And while Eleven's real mother may be staring into space, reliving her government-sponsored trip, at least Joyce is here in *loco parentis*.[2] I know what you're doing, Duffer Brothers! you cry. Yes, Jonathan and Nancy are going to get together and yes, Joyce and Hopper are going to be Eleven's adopted parents! Oh, it's all going to be so lovely! Thank you, Duffer Brothers, thank you!

Damn you, Duffer Brothers.

---

1   Yes, yes, she may be back in season two, don't be picky.

2   Sadly not Latin for 'my parents are crazy'.

FAMILIAR THINGS

There's a moment in the opening bike chase where we wonder if we're about to see another direct homage to *E.T. The Extra-Terrestrial*. As the kids speed towards the Hawkins Power and Light van, could Eleven be about to make their bikes fly so they can escape the seemingly inevitable collision? No. The moment is subverted and it ends up being the van that sails through the air.

Not a reference per se, but it's lovely that Dustin's go-to analogy for a traitor is Lando Calrissian, Billy Dee Williams's character from *The Empire Strikes Back* and *Return of the Jedi*. Though we could point out, if we're feeling particularly picky, that Lando swiftly has a change of heart and goes on to earn General stripes for his heroism.

Mr Clarke knows how to show his date a good time; what better movie to get someone in a romantic mood than John Carpenter's *The Thing*?[3]

The notion of sensory deprivation tanks increasing one's mental powers is a common one, seen in Ken Russell's drug-fuellled *Altered States* (1980), Spielberg's *Minority Report* (2002) and the TV series *Fringe*,[4] to name just three examples. Perhaps the Duffer Brothers were intentionally referencing the first two, perhaps the idea has just become a sci-fi staple.

When Eleven finds Barb in the Upside Down she's not

---

3   Maybe *Driller Killer* (1979), that would charm anyone.

4   You've had a couple of chapters to catch up, if you STILL haven't seen it I'm livid with you.

looking at her best; we'll talk about *Alien* next time so I'll instead mention the British movie *Inseminoid*, a 1981 picture that also revolves around the notion of alien creatures impregnating human hosts. Director Norman J. Warren[5] insists that *Alien* didn't influence his movie (despite it being released a couple of years earlier) but I offer it for your viewing 'pleasure' if you decide *Alien* isn't quite cheap and sleazy enough.

STRANGER SOUNDS

Only one tune to note for this episode but it's one of special interest and it's used twice. Firstly, when Mike, Dustin and Lucas try to explain the Upside Down to Hopper, Joyce, Jonathan and Nancy, then again when they're filling the paddling pool at the school. The track is 'Fields of Coral' from Vangelis, taken from his 1996 album *Oceanic*. The album was nominated for a Grammy Award in the Best New Age Album category.[6]

Evangelos Odysseas Papathanassiou (you can see why he chose to release his work under the name Vangelis) is a Greek legend of electronic music. Most famous for his soundtrack work – particularly his scores for *Chariots of*

---

5   Also responsible for the fun *Satan's Slave* (1976), *Prey* (1977) and *Terror* (1978).
6   Alongside *Le Roi est mort, vive le Roi!* by Enigma, *Voyager* from Mike Oldfield, *Canyon Lullaby* by Paul Winter and Michael Hedges' album *Oracle*. The latter won.

Fire (1981)[7] and *Blade Runner* (1982) – he has released more than fifty albums.

Vangelis was interested in music from a very early age, though always avoided traditional training; he is entirely self-taught and never learned to read sheet music. Throughout the sixties he formed a couple of bands, playing mainly progressive rock music, but it was during the seventies that his career as an electronica solo artist took flight. Throughout said career he has alternated between soundtrack composition and original work and his influence cannot be understated. He has received several honours in his lifetime, including having a small planet named after him in 1995 and a Public Service Medal from NASA in 2003.

As a side note, the music cue when the two cars of agents arrive at the kids' derelict bus hideout is SO John Carpenter it may as well have been commissioned to direct a remake of *The Fog*.

HONOURABLE STRANGERS

We've avoided them far too long, it's time we looked to the people behind the worst friends a Steve Harrington could have: Chester Rushing and Chelsea Talmadge, otherwise known as Tommy and Carol.

Chelsea Talmadge became interested in theatre at the age of twelve, having attended an entertainment summer

---

7   Which won the Academy Award for Best Original Score.

camp.[8] 2016 was her breakout year: not only did she play Carol in *Stranger Things*, she appeared in *Still the King*, the comedy show co-created by (and starring) Billy Ray Cyrus. The show concerns a washed-up country singer turned Elvis impersonator who discovers he has a daughter from a one-night stand. Talmadge plays Mabel, the daughter's best friend. She filmed both shows at the same time and will next be seen in period medical drama *Mercy Street*.

Rushing was born in Texas but spent a lot of his childhood moving around, as his father worked in the oil industry. He clocked up homes in nine different countries including Saudi Arabia, Egypt, Romania and France. As an actor, he has appeared in TV shows such as *South of Hell* and *NCIS: New Orleans* as well as a number of movies including the horror pictures *Don't Look in the Basement 2* (2015) and *Cold Moon* (2016). He also appears in the new Wolverine movie, *Logan*, due to be released in 2017.

Rushing is an accomplished musician; his album *Halfway Across the Stars* is available and his song 'Paint the World' was sampled by EDM artists Jidax and Enzo Darren.

Because he's far lovelier than Tommy, he also works with autistic children and those with learning differences, providing musical therapy.

---

8   Which sounds like a combination of old UK sitcom *Hi-De-Hi* and *Friday the 13th*, a mental image I will now be obsessed with.

HOMEWORK

1. Where does Lucas tell Dustin to meet him during the opening chase?

2. When discussing Eleven with Agent Frasier, what does Mike's dad worry she might be?

3. How much does Steve's bottle of aspirin and can of Coke cost?

4. What's the license plate number of Steve's car?

5. Mr Clarke's date is horrified at the sight of Charles Hallahan's gloopy, separating head in John Carpenter's The Thing. What does Mr Clarke tell her the filmmakers used to achieve the effect?

6. What does Dustin tell Mr Clarke his sensory deprivation tank will be for?

7. What did the boys last use the inflatable paddling pool for?

8. How much salt will they need?

9. How does Dustin check to see if they've added enough salt to the water?

10. What extra item does Nancy steal from the police station?

ADDITIONAL RESEARCH

Watch *Fringe*, because this gap in your knowledge has gone on too long. If you've already seen it, force someone else to watch it. Then shout, "Where were you when we needed you? We could have had a couple more seasons of this if you'd shown up on time!"

NOTES

THE DNA OF STRANGER THINGS: THE LOOK OF THE SHOW

Whoever first said 'don't judge a book by its cover' was, of course, an idiot.[9] It's what covers are for. They are there to set the tone, to intrigue and tantalise, to lure you in. They are there to give you a clue as to whether the book is your sort of thing. In TV terms, this peripheral aesthetic lure is usually found in the show's logo and advertising.

The Duffer Brothers' urge to channel the eighties certainly extended through all parts of the production.

BENGUIAT

The title logo is designed in a modified version of the Benguiat font, released through the International Typeface Corporation and designed by Ed Benguiat. Benguiat is a big deal in the world of typography – one of those arts that few think about but all would miss – and has designed over six hundred fonts during his career. He also designed an amazing number of logos including (and this really is only a handful of the many you would know) the distinctive blue

---

9   It's no good, I can't find out who did say it first - though it was mentioned in George Eliot's *Mill on the Floss* written in 1860, so whoever it was, they're a long dead idiot and can't come after us for a fight. Oh, and, yes, I get that's generally an expression used to define people not books but it's still a poor analogy because it hinges on the book part being true for the analogy to work. And it doesn't. So there.

oval of Ford cars, the bunny-adorned *Playboy*, the suave *Esquire* magazine and even the masthead of *The New York Times*. He also created the logo for the *Planet of the Apes* movie series and the green-neon fringed lettering of David Lynch's *Twin Peaks*.

The Benguiat font was used on a number of Steven King novels in the eighties, and it was that association that design company Imaginary Forces wanted to channel for the *Stranger Things* logo. The degree with which the public at large took it to heart can be seen in the popularity of the 'Make It Stranger' online typeface generator created by branding company Nelson Cash.[10]

GREENBERG

But a logo is only part of a title sequence. In the case of *Stranger Things*, of course, a big part because, inspired by the work of Richard Greenberg, the logo itself is the focus. Richard Greenberg designed title sequences for a number of movies that will already be familiar from previous sections, including *Alien, The Dead Zone, Altered States* and *Blow Out*. In most cases, Greenberg chose to let the logo do the talking, the slow build of the A L I E N and – particularly close to *Stranger Things* – the piecing together of *The Dead Zone* logo, layering over the opening shots of the movie. Imaginary Forces actually started work on the titles before the show was even shot, moving through various different

---

10   http://makeitstranger.com

takes on the brief – and different fonts – before it became the version we know now.

STRUZAN

But if we're really looking for the 'cover' to *Stranger Things*, it's Kyle Lambert's poster image. It harkens back to the days of painted poster art, particularly the work of Drew Struzan.

Struzan painted posters for the Indiana Jones movies, *Blade Runner, Back to the Future, The Thing, The Goonies* and a host of others. Flipping through his portfolio makes you wonder if he painted the poster for every single damn one of the movies you loved of the period.

Artist Kyle Lambert immediately honed in on Struzan's work as something he wanted to evoke. The Duffer Brothers commissioned him to create six pieces of art that would be given to the cast as gifts, and working on this helped him hone the look he was going for.

CHAPTER EIGHT

THE UPSIDE DOWN

O h Hopper, what have you done? In truth, whatever he had to in order to find Will and keep himself and Joyce alive. Mike may have trouble forgiving him – if he ever finds out – but we can surely understand. If they live to tell the tale, that is; Dr Brenner certainly doesn't think they will and, as Hopper and Joyce plod through the set of *Alien*, we think he may have a point. At least they don't have the Demogorgon to worry about, eh? Because, look, he's popped by the Byers house for a play on Will's yo-yo.

Steve picked the wrong day to turn out to be nice, didn't he? Perhaps not, as it certainly earns him brownie points, with Nancy *and* us. His Han-Solo-at-the-end-of-*Star-Wars* moment is lovely, jolly TV.

Look, I know I've mentioned this before but Steve being an actual, fully-rounded human being – and a decent one at that – is one of the best aspects of the show. Obviously we're rooting for Jonathan a wee bit, how can we not? But, soppy old sod that I am, I find myself hoping he'll simply have found a different girlfriend by the time season two rolls around, possibly someone with dyed-black hair and the sort of dopey eyes that can only mean hours of Joy Division have been pumped into her ears. That way, everyone's a winner.

Sadly, Nancy, Jonathan and Steve end up trashing the house but not helping all that much. The Demogorgon has blood in its nostrils and a Dr Brenner to chew. Or does he? On one hand, we may be being spared the violent death of Mathew Modine – call me sick if you will but I think Brenner is the sort of villain that we deserve to see a few spilled entrails of, it's Horror Movie Rule 57, let the bad guy's death *linger* – or he's not dead at all and that white hair will come back to haunt us again.

And look! Mike and Eleven are going to be a thing! How sweet! He's even going to take her to the … Oh.

Duffer Brothers, come here, I wish to tug firmly on your beards.

(But, hey, there's another series, we know this isn't the end of Eleven, we can bear a tearful goodbye for now).

And it's all over. Except for the bits that aren't. What's Hopper up to? How broken is Will Byers? Will Karen Wheeler ever leave Ted? There she is, look, drinking a glass of wine while Ted sleeps in the La-Z-Boy. Of course she is. I bet it's not her first glass and it won't be her last.

FAMILIAR THINGS

You have to love a 'getting ready to beat up horrible things' montage sequence such as the one we have with Jonathan and Nancy here. Again, it's such a common dramatic beat in this kind of story that I doubt it's referencing *Nightmare on Elm Street* explicitly but, as I haven't mentioned it yet, and we know that the Duffer Brothers consider Wes Craven an influence on the show, maybe it's time I did.

Certainly parallels could be drawn between the dream world stalked by the blade-fingered loon Freddy Krueger – a dimension outside our own but one you can be dragged into and die in – and the Upside Down. Plus of course, there's the fact the hero of the original movie (and indeed the third)[1] is also called Nancy. Towards the end of the first movie, Nancy Thompson prepares for battle much as our heroes do here. *Home Alone* but with more bleeding.

Craven's movie so nearly didn't get made at all. He'd already made a name for himself with *The Last House on the Left* (1972) and *The Hills Have Eyes* (1977) but his career was in something of a slump after a string of lesser movies. He wrote the script and shopped it around, receiving rejections left right and centre. At one point the only studio interested was Walt Disney, but they wanted him to tone it down so it was suitable for a young audience (shades of the Duffer Brothers pitching *Stranger Things* here for sure). Craven didn't want to. Thank God.

Finally, New Line Cinema, who up until that point had only distributed movies, not stumped up the cash to make any, saved the day. Even then, investment fell through during shooting, with cast and crew going unpaid for a fortnight until more money was secured. On such humble tales are franchises built. The *Nightmare on Elm Street* movies went on to make a fortune, and New Line Cinema made a lot more movies. As did Craven, including, of course, another hugely successful franchise in the *Scream* movies.[2]

---

1   Actress Heather Langenkamp also appeared in the seventh movie, the groundbreaking *Wes Craven's New Nightmare* (1999) but she wasn't playing Nancy, she was playing herself, as the movie had an entirely post-modern riff suggesting that the cinematic version of Freddy Krueger was actually inspired by a real demon, one that is emerging into the real world, released from his fictional prison now that they'd stopped making the movies.

2   Two in one career is frankly staggering and a testament to Craven's ability to form witty and clever horror movies that also had a popular touch.

We also really need to talk about *Alien* (1979) because the look of Ridley Scott's movie is a huge influence on the monstrous elements of *Stranger Things*. Never is this more obvious than when Hopper and Joyce find what appears to be a translucent egg sac while they're looking for Will. It bears more than a passing similarity to the egg sacs laid by the creatures in the *Alien* films, out of which are hatched face-hugging creatures that shove a gooey protuberance in your mouth in which they lay spore ... sound familiar?

Scott worked with Swiss artist H. R. Giger on all the alien aspects of the movie (the human elements being handled by Ron Cobb and Chris Foss) and it is Giger's organic, grotesquery that can be felt in the Upside Down, a surfeit of slick, veined horrible.

When it comes to the design of the Demogorgon itself, while there are certainly elements of Giger's Alien, its unfolding mouth and spindly limbs, we can taste a few pinches of Guillermo Del Toro too, particularly in the pale, slender creations found in his movie *Pan's Labyrinth*.

STRANGER SOUNDS

And it's a welcome return to those Germanic keyboard tinkerers, Tangerine Dream with their track 'Horizon' (specifically the Warsaw Gate Mix). The piece was originally featured on their 1984 live album, Poland.

When Hopper and Joyce fight to resuscitate Will, we hear the song 'When It's Cold I'd Like to Die' by Moby, the stage name of Richard Melville Hall. The track comes from his third album *Everything is Wrong*, released in 1995.

As we move from the police station Christmas party to Hopper's illicit food drop, we have the seasonal warbling of the Mormon Tabernacle Choir singing 'Carol of the Bells'. The Mormon Tabernacle Choir has 360 members and is one of the most famous choirs in the world, their albums having frequently topped the classical charts. 'Carol of the Bells' was composed by the Ukrainian Mykola Leontovych in 1914, based on a Ukranian folk chant. During the recent Guy Adams Award for Creepiest Christmas Carol it won first place.

Fir ally, playing under all the Christmas cheer and slug vomi ing at the Byers house, we have the old Bing Crosby standard 'White Christmas'. Written by Irving Berlin in 1942 it is the most-recorded Christmas song of all time with over five hundred versions recorded. The Bing Crosby version is the biggest selling single of all time.[3]

HONOURABLE STRANGERS

Fine, we'll talk about her. When not killing Benny … no, sorry, I just need a minute, I liked Benny, Benny was nice … (BREATHES IN) … Catherine Dyer has appeared in a number of TV shows and movies, including 2009's American Football biopic *The Blind Side* and 2016's *Dirty Grandpa*.

---

3   Although there is some controversy, due to the fact that it was released before chart statistics began to be compiled in 1955. The best-selling single released *since* 1955 is Elton John's 'Candle in the Wind 1997', recorded as a tribute to Diana, Princess of Wales.

She also works a great deal on the other side of the camera. In the mid-nineties she became Development Assistant for Lifetime Television's Original Movies Department, moving to A&E television a couple of years later to become Programming Co-Ordinator for their does-exactly-what you'd-think-given-the-title show *Biography*. This led eventually to her becoming Manager of Documentary Programming and Supervising Producer for the channel, with *Biography* earning a Primetime Emmy nomination in 2003.

In an attempt to charm us into forgetting her Benny-killing ways she is the author of a cookbook, *You Want Me to Bring A Dish?* Yeah, Dyer, you probably stole it from Benny's kitchen, you psycho.

Her favourite movies (according to a Reddit appearance) are *Goodfellas*, *Rear Window* and *Airplane*. So at least she has taste.

HOMEWORK

Your final quiz! Don't complain if it's a bit silly, this was a nightmare episode to find questions for.

1. There's a yo-yo prominently featured in Will's room. What design does it have on it?

2. What book does Hopper read to his daughter from?

3. What dessert does Dustin raid the school kitchen for?

4. What time is it when Eleven kills the Demogorgon?

5. And what is the last thing she says?

6. What's the first thing Will Byers says on waking?

7. What has Jonathan made for him?

8. What is Eleven's favourite food?

9. What monster is Will forced to face in Mike's new campaign?

10. The final question in the whole book and what am I reduced to? SIGH. What's wrong with Joyce's mashed potatoes?

ADDITIONAL RESEARCH

Learn how to make decent mashed potatoes.

NOTES

APENDIX 1

HARDLY STRANGERS

W ho were all those people? We spent so long
with them I think it's time we found out. In
alphabetical order (see, it's not just because I'm
obsessed with Karen Wheeler), a rundown of the main cast
of the show:

CARA BUONO – Karen Wheeler

Buono is a New Yorker of Italian descent. An actor, writer
and director, well known for her roles in both *The Sopranos*
and *Mad Men*. Genre credits include: yet another mother not
entirely aware of quite what horrors her son is brushing up
against in *Let Me In* (2010), the English-language remake of
the masterful Swedish novel and movie *Let the Right One In*;
a recurring role in the TV adaptation of Stephen King's *The
Dead Zone,* as Anna Turner (2008); Bruce Banner's mum
Edith when he looked like Eric Bana rather than Mark Ruffalo
in Ang Lee's ill-received (but what do they know?) *Hulk* (2003)
and – terribly obscure one this – a bored housewife who ends
up assisting aliens (and fixing her love life) in Barry Strugatz's
well-meaning but flawed sci-fi comedy *From Other Worlds*
(2004).

MILLIE BOBBY BROWN – Eleven

Born in Marbella, Spain to English parents, Brown moved to
the UK at the age of four, living in Bournemouth. Her family
emigrated again when she was eight, this time to Florida to
launch a tooth-whitening business.

Brown signed up for a weekend stage school and was
picked up by an agent who saw her perform. When the agent
told Brown's family that they should move to Hollywood, they

took a gamble and did so. It didn't work out. Despite a handful of jobs coming her way,[1] the family ran out of money and were forced to move back to the UK.

Brown, disconsolate and assuming she would never get anywhere in the business attended an audition for a casting agent which didn't go well. Tearful and despondent, she had one more audition that day: *Stranger Things*. When asked to cry in the audition she found it all too easy. She got the job. Obviously.

JOE CHREST – Ted Wheeler

"What did I do?" asks Mike's dad as he finds himself sat alone at the dinner table in the first episode of *Stranger Things*. The answer is: a fair bit, frankly.

A United States Air Force veteran where, slightly terrifyingly, he earned commendations for Cold War service and expert marksmanship (perhaps I shouldn't have mocked Ted Wheeler, as the actor playing him could kill me from a distance), Chrest holds both a BFA and MFA degree[2] in directing and is a founding member of the Swine Palace theatre in Louisiana and the founding artistic director of Ignition Film Repertory Company, which is dedicated to producing original works for the screen.

As an actor his credits are extensive, from recurring roles in shows like *True Detective* and *Treme* to appearances in movies

---

1   Including a starring role in *Intruders,* the BBC America TV show adapted from Michael Marshall Smith's novel of the same name. A book that all fans of *Stranger Things* should seek out, as it's wonderful and right up their street. Now. I mean it. Go. Buy. Read.

2   Bachelor of Fine Arts and Master of Fine Arts.

such as *Ant Man*, *21 Jump Street* (and its sequel) and the catchily-titled *The Hunger Games: Mockingjay – Part 2*.

Bonus genre appearance for further homework: Chrest appeared as a villain in the first season of *Millennium*, the follow-up show from *The X-Files*'s Chris Carter. He'll be the one masturbating while he watches a bomb he's just planted explode. *Millennium* is a clever and subversive horror fantasy show that is certainly worth your time, most particularly its deliriously nuts second season.

NATALIA DYER – Nancy Wheeler

Natalia Dyer started acting at the age of twelve, appearing in Disney's *Hannah Montana - The Movie* (2009). 2011 saw her work with Aidan Quinn, Brooke Shields and Kris Kristofferson in *The Greening of Whitney Brown*, a somewhat saccharine tale of a rich girl forced to realise what's important in life by spending time with a horse. *Blue Like Jazz* followed in 2012, an adaptation of a semi-autobiographical Christian memoir by Donald Miller. The movie was partially funded through Kickstarter after an investor backed out. One of the most successful campaigns of the year, with nearly three hundred and fifty thousand dollars being raised, director Steve Taylor possibly regretted his gracious offer to personally call every backer who contributed ten dollars or over on the phone as it took him over a year to do so.

It was 2014's *I Believe in Unicorns* that gave Dyer a role to really sink her teeth into. The coming-of-age movie featured Dyer in the lead and saw her gain a plethora of good notices with Brain Tallerico of RogerEbert.com saying: "… the film simply wouldn't work at all without the committed, fantastic performance of Natalie Dyer. She balances the innocence and desire of her character in perfectly equal measures, sketching a person in that dangerous part of life in which they are not a child and yet also not quite yet a woman. She holds every scene, adding emotional weight to clichés that would have been paper-thin without her work."

Currently she is studying at New York University's Gallatin School of Individualized Study, a school specialising, as the name suggests, in a more individual course program devised by the students themselves. Notable alumni include: Isabella Rossini, Anne Hathaway and Rooney Mara.

DAVID HARBOUR – Jim Hopper

David Harbour is a New Yorker who received his acting break in 1999 playing a farmhand in a Broadway revival of N. Richard Nash's play *The Rainmaker*. His theatre career included a 2005 Tony Award for Best Actor in a Featured Role (Play) for his performance as Nick in a 2005 revival of the Edward Albee play *Who's Afraid of Virginia Woolf?*

Onscreen, he has had recurring roles in TV shows such as *Pan Am*, *The Newsroom* and *State of Affairs,* as well as appearing in many movies.

Fans of watching a man in a dinner suit punch people will recognise him in 2008's *Quantum of Solace*, the second of Daniel Craig's appearances as James Bond. Harbour can be found beneath a moustache as dodgy as the character he's playing, a CIA section chief striking an illicit deal with the film's villain in order to allow the US access to Bolivian oil. Such underhand dealing would never happen in real life. Obviously.

RANDALL P. HAVENS – Scott Clarke

Not only is Mr Clarke the nicest science teacher in the world, he plays John Carpenter's *The Thing* to get his girlfriend in the mood. Because nothing opens someone's curiosity door quite like watching a severed head grow legs and try to kill Kurt Russell.

Actor Randall P. Havens (usually credited as the rather less formal Randy Havens)[3] has appeared in numerous TV shows, including the animated comedy *Archer*, *The Vampire Diaries* and *Halt and Catch Fire*. The latter is of particular interest, not only because it charts the rise of the personal computer in the eighties but because it's the show Havens grew that luxuriant moustache for.

CHARLIE HEATON – Jonathan Byers

Heaton is an English actor, born in Bridlington, East Yorkshire.[4]

Moving to London when he was sixteen, he became a drummer for noise-rock band Comanechi.[5] With Akiko Matsuura on vocals and Simon Petrovitch on guitar, the trio went on a world tour for a year. To see Heaton in stick-flinging action head here: https://youtu.be/LIIqMTZjRlc

On his return, short of money, his sister suggested he try

---

3   Maybe he relishes sounding like a place you might hold sexual orgies? I certainly would. Maybe the publisher's legal team will cut this joke, even though I hid it so well in a footnote?

4   Where I spent many a dull Sunday as a child, sitting on a beach staring at ill donkeys. Yes, I appreciate you didn't really need to know that.

5   A genre of music blending traditional rock instrumentation with the atonal, dissonant sounds of the avant-garde. Much like *Stranger Things*, it has its roots in the eighties.

his luck enrolling with a commercial talent agency, which led to a commercial for a Swiss insurance company. Film roles followed, including the indie picture *As You Are*, which won the Special Jury Award at the 216 Sundance festival.

On television, he was mainly to be found in close proximity to corpses and coppers with an appearance in the UK crime dramas *DCI Banks* and *Vera*. After that he ticked *Casualty* off his list, as all British actors eventually must.[6]

JOE KEERY – Steve Harrington

Joe Keery is also a musician, guitarist/vocalist for Post Animal, a garage rock band from Chicago.

As an actor, *Stranger Things* is certainly the role that will make him, though he's appeared in a handful of other TV shows as well as the movies *Harry Gamble's Birthday Party* (2015) and *The Charnel House* (2016).

Not everything on the Internet is true, though if enough people believe something it may as well be. A jolly fan theory based on the similarity between Keery and *Parks and Recreation* actor Ben Schwartz suggested that their characters were father and son. The sitcom creator Michael Schur was happy to sign off on such silliness and the genetic link was made 'official' via a comedy sketch on *The Late, Late Show with James Corden*.

---

6   For non-UK readers, *Casualty* is a long running medical drama/soap that chews through actors remorselessly as they're thrown off ladders, hit by cars or caught in the middle of a bizarre industrial accident on their inevitable path towards a hospital bed and a few scenes shared with the regular cast.

GATEN MATARAZZO – Dustin Henderson

Stranger Things is only Matarazzo's second onscreen acting role (the first being an appearance during the second season of NBC's *James Spader Has Fun Hour*, or *The Blacklist* as it's also known). He has a couple of significant theatre credits, however, having appeared in both *Priscilla, Queen of the Desert* (in 2011) and *Les Misérables* (in 2014). In the latter, he appeared on Broadway before touring for six months playing the part of Gavroche, a wily little street urchin.[7] In an interview with Vincent Jackson for Pressofatlanticcity.com Matarazzo, aged ten, admitted, "Gavroche has been my dream role since I was seven." Which is just so adorable I have to mention it.

His sister, Sabrina – four years his senior – also sings and acts and encouraged Matarazzo into the profession. They sang together in 2009 at the US Open tennis tournament.

Matarazzo originally auditioned for the role of Mike but was told he didn't look demanding enough, so ended up reading Lucas's lines before being cast as Dustin![8]

Matarazzo has cleidocranial dysplasia, a congenital disorder that affects the development of bones and teeth. While Matarazzo's form of the condition is mild, he has no collarbones and his teeth never fully developed so he wears false ones. He hopes that his appearance on the show will

---

7   SPOILER: Mini, loveable Gavroche comes a cropper in the second act of the play when he's shot by soldiers. This, awful, awful writer was struck by a fit of the giggles when watching the scene during the London production of the show. This earned him actual death threats from the tearful audience members near him and a reprimand from theatre staff.

8   As Matarazzo explained to Ben Travers at indiewire.com.

raise awareness of cleidocranial dysplasia and encourage others with the condition to feel more comfortable about their appearance.

CALEB McLAUGHLIN – Lucas Sinclair

Like Matarazzo, Caleb McLaughlin started his career on the Broadway stage. He trained in dance at The Harlem School of Arts (and freely admits that he can't stop dancing, frequently busting out moves for the sheer hell of it) going on to appear as Young Simba in a production of *The Lion King*. A run of appearances in TV shows followed: *Law & Order: Special Victims Unit*, *Forever* and *Unforgettable* then a recurring role in NBC cop show *Shades of Blue*.

When his agent secured him an audition for *Stranger Things*, he auditioned three times in New York before flying to Los Angeles to meet the Duffer Brothers, who offered him the part. He had already known Gaten Matarazzo for three years before they filmed together, the two having met during their time on Broadway. They weren't appearing in the same shows, but met at a nearby park where a lot of the kids appearing on Broadway would hang out when not working.

As well as, obviously, filming the second series of *Stranger Things*, McLaughlin went on to appear in *The New Edition Story*, a miniseries based on the rise to success of the American boyband. He appears as the young Ricky Bell, one of the founding members of the group.

MATHEW MODINE – Martin Brenner

Modine grew up in cinema; his father, Mark Alexander Modine, managed drive-in theatres.[9] The large family (Modine has seven siblings) moved frequently as the land the theatres were on was often deemed more valuable as real estate than as a cinema.

Moving to New York after he graduated, Modine went on to appear in a number of seminal movies including Alan Parker's *Birdy* (1984) and Stanley Kubrick's *Full Metal Jacket* (1987).[10] He also appeared in John Schlesinger's 1990 thriller *Pacific Heights*, which I mention purely because it's brilliant and you should all watch it.

He famously turned down the part of 'Maverick' Mitchell in 1986's *Top Gun* as he didn't agree with the film's pro-military stance. Good for him. Tom Cruise took the part instead and we all know how that worked out.

Modine is also well known for his environmental activism

---

9   Accepting that the drive-in is now as lost to time as a good deal of the trappings of *Stranger Things*, perhaps I'd better explain. Drive-in theatres were exactly what they sound like, large open-air lots where patrons would drive up, park, grab a – usually godawful – wired speaker from a wooden post next to the parking space, bring it in through the window and watch movies projected on a massive screen. Later, they became so advanced as to broadcast the movie soundtrack on AM or FM radio (I haven't time to explain to you what they are, just roll with it) so you could tune your car radio in and listen through your own speakers. They reached the height of their success in the fifties in America, but experienced a resurgence of interest in the seventies when they began showing exploitation movies such as 1977's *Drive-In Massacre* (down-at-heel carnival turns itself into a drive-in theatre to make more money; when patrons end up being murdered with a sabre, could the onetime sword swallower be the culprit?).

10   As well as the odd well-meaning flop of course, what great actor hasn't? While I'm not one who relishes being negative, 1995's pirate action picture *Cutthroat Island* is perhaps notable enough to mention. The movie had a troubled production and stands as one of the biggest box-office flops of all time. This is not, of course, Modine's fault.

and his promotion of the bicycle as a mode of transport.

ANNISTON & TINSLEY PRICE – Holly Wheeler
Right, fine, so maybe Mike's kid sister isn't exactly a main
character but the twins who play her share another genre
TV credit so I'm mentioning them anyway. They are one of
the number of children to have played Judith Grimes, baby
daughter and constant potential zombie amuse-bouche to Rick
(or was it Shane?) and Lori in AMC's *The Walking Dead*.

SHANNON PURSER – Barbara Holland
In the eighties, becoming viral was something to be feared; not
anymore.

Purser has always enjoyed acting, performing in small-
scale theatre, which led to her getting picked up by an agent.
A couple of years of auditioning and meeting with casting
directors didn't lead to work – as, it so often doesn't in that
competitive and fickle business. Then her agent got a call about
Stranger Things. Purser sent in a taped audition, which led to
her being called in to read for the Duffer Brothers.

Shortly after, she was sat in a movie theatre with her mum.
She checked her emails on her phone and discovered she'd got
the job.[11] Her very first onscreen role.

The fact that her character in general and Purser's
performance in particular won the viewer's hearts has led
to lots more opportunities, including being cast in The CW's
Riverdale.

---

11   A cinema crime but we'll let it pass. Interestingly, Purser might not be so
     lenient as she worked in a movie theatre.

WINONA RYDER – Joyce Byers

Winona Ryder was born Winona Laura Horowitz. The Winona came from the Minnesotan town near where she was born, whereas the Laura was in honour of Laura Huxley, friend of Ryder's parents and wife of novelist Aldous Huxley. Her godfather is Dr Timothy Leary, the renowned psychologist and writer who controversially advocated the therapeutic potential of psychedelic drugs such as LSD and psilocybin.[12] Family friends also included beat poet Allan Ginsberg and novelist Philip K. Dick.[13]

Ryder began acting at the age of twelve, making her first movie appearance in 1986 in *Lucas*, starring Corey Haim.[14] It was her appearance in two 1988 movies that thoroughly cemented her stardom. Firstly, her wonderfully dry Goth turn in Tim Burton's *Beetlejuice* then her murderous turn alongside Christian Slater in *Heathers*.

Countless great roles followed, from reuniting with Tim Burton (and appearing alongside Johnny Depp, whom she was engaged to at the time) in *Edward Scissorhands* (1990) to

---

12   Unsurprisingly given his drug use, Leary was arrested countless times and was once described by US President Richard Nixon as "the most dangerous man in America". Now that's what I call a godfather.

13   Who must also be on every *Stranger Things* fan's reading list. While he is most often remembered for writing novels that became highly successful movies (not least *Blade Runner*, based on Dick's far-better-titled *Do Androids Dream of Electric Sheep?*), those movies rarely do justice to the raw power and imagination of his original work.

14   Perhaps the most obvious poster boy for eighties cinema were it not for the tragic turn his life took. He died, destitute and depressed, of a drug overdose at the young age of thirty-eight. Probably most famous for his lead role in revisionist vampire horror comedy *The Lost Boys* (1987), he was a charming presence in a great number of other movies, a couple of which will be mentioned in a few pages' time.

her award-nominated performances in *Little Women* (1994) and James Mangold's 1999 thriller *Girl, Interrupted* (which she also executive produced).

NOAH SCHNAPP – Will Byers

Schnapp saw the musical *Annie* on Broadway at the age of six and left the theatre crying because he realised how much he wanted to be on the stage. He started working professionally two years later and ended up landing a gig with Steven Spielberg (as Tom Hanks's son in 2015's *Bridge of Spies*) a year later. Go Schnapp.

He also voiced that perennial comic dreamer, the long-suffering Charlie Brown in *The Peanuts Movie*. He credits following the advice of his mother as the reason he got that job, having spent days before the audition watching old *Peanuts* cartoons to get a handle on how Charlie Brown spoke.

MARK STEGER – The Demogorgon

He may never speak but how can we ignore Mark Steger?

Steger, a dancer and choreographer as well as actor, first brushed up against the monstrous through his experimental dance performance group Osseus Labrynt who would perform naked in unusual locations.[15]

Having been introduced to the metal band Tool, Steger

---

15   Don't try this at home; when Steger does it it's art, for you it may simply be an arrestable offence.

worked with guitarist Adam Jones[16] to create a creepy music video for the band's song Schism.

He then went on to work on *American Horror Story*, choreographing sections for the third series of the show and then appearing as the slick, horrid 'Addiction Demon' in the fifth series.

A note given to Steger by the Duffer Brothers particularly struck home. They described the Demogorgon as being like the shark from *Jaws*, something that remained hidden much of the time, only to emerge, raw and hungry when it needed to feed.

FINN WOLFHARD – Mike Wheeler

Wolfhard has appeared in a couple of independent movies, a handful of music videos and the shows *The 100* and *Supernatural,* but it was *Stranger Things* he was arguably born for. Unlike the rest of the young cast, Wolfhard was already up to speed on a lot of the eighties movies the show would riff off. His father, pursuing a career as a screenwriter,[17] watched a lot of movies for inspiration and showed Wolfhard *E.T. The Extra-Terrestrial* when he was two! Wolfhard continued to dip his toes, both with his brother and father, and considers *The Goonies* one of his favourite movies. In fact, it's the fact that he is 'obsessed with retro '80s movies' that made his agent first

---

16   Jones had previously worked for the famous Stan Winston special effects workshop, where he helped create monsters for movies such as *Predator 2*, *Jurassic Park, Terminator 2: Judgment Day* and the fourth and fifth *Nightmare on Elm Street* sequels.

17   Something that, utterly adorably, his son is now hoping to help happen through his own success!

suggest the casting as they felt – quite rightly, as we can all now agree – that the part was perfect for him.

He auditioned and was then invited to have a Skype call with the Duffer Brothers, during which they apparently discussed nothing else but what movies they all liked.

Wolfhard's enthusiasm and knowledge clearly shone through as they invited him over to LA to perform another audition. Then, a month later, one more. Finally, after a further month of waiting he got the call from Matt Duffer telling him the part was his. Wolfhard is convinced a big part of why he was cast is because, "I'm basically [The Duffer Brothers] as a kid."[18]

---

18   As said to Jen Chaney for Vulture.com.

APENDIX 2

EVEN STRANGER SOUNDS

So, you've worn out Kyle Dixon and Michael Stein's soundtrack[1] but need some more aural goodness to keep you fed? I'm happy to help. A mixture of vintage tunes and modern, electronic soundtracks, I am happy to give your iTunes account a thrashing.

Tron - Legacy (Daft Punk)

The French, helmet wearing, Daft Punk can be a trifle hit and miss in my opinion, with a number of their tracks starting wonderfully then going on precisely three times longer than you want them to. Their 2013 album *Random Access Memories* (mentioned earlier when we were discussing Giorgio Moroder) is a worthy exception, but their soundtrack to 2010's *Tron* sequel is simply a revelation. Bristling with epic, soaring melodies, a warm blend between the orchestral and the electronic it contains huge worlds of expression and, like all the best movie soundtracks, delivers an experience that stands entirely on its own.

Maniac (Rob)

Franck Khalfoun's remake of the eighties slasher movie shows its roots in its soundtrack, composed and performed by Robin Coudert, a French musician who works under the professional name Rob. A swirling neon of synths combine with pulsing rhythms and delicate, beautiful melodies. Like the work of Kyle Dixon and Michael Stein, it manages to be both eerie and

---

1   No, obviously you can't wear out a soundtrack, especially not an MP3; believe me, I've tried, particularly with a number of the entries on this list.

yet surprisingly warm; it's music for a city at night, a city that has bad things in it.

Lost Themes (John Carpenter)

Having given Carpenter more than enough space I considered leaving him off this list, then, listening to his 2015 studio album *Lost Themes*, decided I simply had to give it another push.

It's Carpenter's first album of original compositions but that simply frees him up from the narrative of a movie score. Each of the nine tracks here (fifteen if you get the expanded version that includes extra remixes) pulses with energy, showing that Carpenter hasn't lost an ounce of power over the years.

Phantasm (Fred Myrow & Malcolm Seagrave)

Finally, I stop recommending new music to you. The soundtrack to 1979's *Phantasm* sees two classically trained composers put their prog rock and synth hats on for a trippy, eerie selection of music that combines organ, piano and conventional rock sounds with electronica to deliver something unearthly and impossible to forget, much like the movie itself.

The Entity (Charles Bernstein)

Charles Bernstein's career as a composer is long and illustrious, and he'll always have a place in a horror fan's heart as the man that gave us the sigh and piano theme for the original *Nightmare on Elm Street*. As wonderful as that soundtrack is, *The Entity* is its equal. We open with a piano in its death throes before suddenly the looping combination of strings, piano and synths bring us into the dreamy world of the 1982 movie, the tale of a woman tormented by a ghost.

The Beyond (Fabio Frizzi)
I could put any of Fabio Frizzi's scores on this list, they're all magnificent, but I'll settle for this one, the score to Lucio Fulci's bizarre Lovecraftian zombie picture from 1981. A combination of piano, synth, violins and the funkiest bass in horror, he makes you want to tap your feet even while you're watching plumbers having their eyes gouged out. Look, we're talking Lucio Fulci here, that's just the sort of movies he made, OK?

APENDIX 3

80s MOVIE PLAYLIST

This book, like the show itself, is intentionally packed full of references to movies you should watch. But, as with the previous section on music, I can't resist another list. Books like this need lots of lists. Some of these movies have direct, thematic links to the show, others are just movies whose tone fit well with the world of *Stranger Things* and therefore … Well, I hesitate to say they're films I think you'll like because, look, I'm a film obsessive, I own thousands of movies,[1] movies are my thing and I have learned to my cost that there's no such thing as a surefire hit. I have sat down to force-feed my cinematic babies to friends and family time and again and time and again; I've been told my taste stinks just as often as I've had the joy of adding new converts to a beloved movie. This is just how taste works. You don't all have it.[2]

---

1   Around four thousand, actually. Which, now I think about it, isn't actually normal, is it?

2   Though if any of you watch *The 'Burbs* and dare to dislike it, you're dead to me.

WATCHERS (1988)

Director: Jon Hess

Two specimens escape from a secret research laboratory, one is friendly and heroic, the other terrible and made out of special effects and sharp teeth. Sound familiar? If this isn't valuable homework for a *Stranger Things* fan then I don't know what is. In the case of *Watchers* – based on a novel by Dean Koontz[3] – the friendly escapee isn't a young girl but a golden retriever called Einstein. As a bonus, the movie also contains Michael Ironside, an always reliable screen psycho who enlivened many a low-budget movie in the eighties and nineties (as well as his mind-blowing appearance in David Cronenberg's *Scanners*).

---

3   Exceedingly prolific author of over a hundred suspense, horror and sci-fi novels including the *Odd Thomas* series, concerning a short-order cook who sees dead people. All the time.

TWILIGHT ZONE:
THE MOVIE (1983)

Director: John Landis, Stephen Spielberg,
   Joe Dante, George Miller

As you will have gathered by now,
The Twilight Zone was an anthology series
created by Rod Serling.[4] It ran in the US
between 1959 and 1964.[5] This movie,
though flawed and marred with a horrific
accident during production,[6] features four major directors
offering a story each, all bar the first being direct reworkings
of original episodes. Landis's opening tale is uncomfortable
to watch given the accident (see previous footnote). Steven

---

4   A show that offered a different, completely unrelated story and cast each
     week. A popular format in its time – see also *The Outer Limits*, *Alfred
     Hitchcock Presents* or, in the UK, Roald Dahl's *Tales of the Unexpected* –
     but one that has passed out of favour in recent years. Nowadays the term
     is more usually applied to shows like *American Horror Story,* where each
     season is a new story, but not each episode. One notable exception would
     be Charlie Brooker's *Black Mirror*, a clear stepchild of *The Twilight Zone*.

5   With a couple of revivals, one in 1985 that ran for three seasons and another
     in 2002 that was cancelled after one season.

6   The opening story, a parable on racism, presents William Connor, played
     by veteran character actor Vic Morrow, flung into conflicts of the past to
     learn what it feels like to be oppressed for his religious beliefs or ethnicity.
     In the original script, the character is finally redeemed after rescuing two
     Vietnamese children from an assault on their village by American soldiers.
     The story had to be re-edited after a helicopter, the pilot blinded by
     pyrotechnic special effects, crashed, killing both Morrow and
     the two child actors. While a long-running court case
     cleared the filmmakers of blame in their deaths, it's
     inarguable that knowing their fate casts a pall over
     the whole thing.

Spielberg's tale of pensioners in an old people's home, reverting magically to children at night, is certainly touching if a little mawkish. It's in the final two stories, however, where the film really finds its feet and demands your attention. Joe Dante's tale of a child tormenting his family through cartoons is a grotesque and inventive delight and George Miller's finale, with John Lithgow the only one of an aircraft's passengers that knows there's something on the wing of the plane, is simply perfection.

SILVER BULLET (1985)

Director: Dan Attias (initially Don Coscarelli, for more about whom, see below)

Another appearance from Corey Haim on our list, this time as a wheelchair-bound kid who becomes embroiled in a battle against a werewolf who is picking off residents in a New England town. Adapted by Stephen King from his own novella, the film has had its detractors over the years but personally I think it's a charming, effective and often heart-warming picture. Yes, I appreciate these are strange words to use when describing a movie about a man-wolf eating people but King always was one for sentiment as well as scares.

Gary Busey, now famous for being Slightly Mad Gary Busey, is at his best as Haim's irresponsible, flawed but ultimately heroic uncle and Everett McGill (who will, like Haim, appear again on this list) delivers his all as usual.

PHANTASM (1979)

Yes, it was a year early to truly fit the title of this section but I don't care.

Young musician Jody brings up his kid brother, Mike in a Cosy American Town that, like all Cosy American Towns in horror is far from cosy at all. Now we have that piece of predictable plot out the way I'm willing to bet you won't second-guess anything else in this wondrously off-kilter movie from Don Coscarelli. It includes Space Dwarfs, evil, silver balls of death and a giant looming caretaker (played by the glorious Angus Scrimm) who is sometimes a woman.

For the most part it's an exercise in dreamlike horror, which, like the best nightmares, has little interest in logic or answering the questions its own story poses. It led to four more – equally bizarre – sequels, the final film having been released in 2016, a mere eighteen years after the one preceding it.

It was recently released in a very shiny restored version on Blu-ray thanks to J.J. Abrams, a devoted fan of the movie (he named a character in *Star Wars: The Force Awakens* after it). He had his studio restore the film and its soundtrack and it looks better now than I suspect it ever did.

THE MONSTER SQUAD (1987)

Shane Black, co-writer and director of *Iron Man 3*, used to be known for his witty 'buddy-cop' movies such as the *Lethal Weapon* franchise and *The Long Kiss Goodnight*. In 1987, the same year that the first *Lethal Weapon* movie appeared, he also brought this curious slice of fun nostalgia.

The Monster Squad are a gang of kids obsessed with horror movies; little do they know they're about to live one. Reviving the old Universal Monsters (as Universal is about to do again) the kids face Dracula, the Mummy, the Wolf Man, Frankenstein's monster and the Gillman. It's a strange, slightly uneven movie but when it's fun – as it so frequently is – it shines brightly enough to carry you over the odd speed bump.

THE PEOPLE UNDER THE STAIRS (1991)

While at heart, *The Monster Club* is a kids' movie, *The People Under the Stairs* just feels as if it could be, if it weren't for the cannibals and the sight of Everett McGill in his S&M gear.

Written and directed by Wes Craven, it's probably his most under-discussed movie, possibly because it refuses to place itself in any conventional boxes.

'Fool' Williams, a young kid whose family are about to be evicted from their home by their grotesque landlords (Everett McGill and Wendy Robie, reunited from David Lynch's *Twin Peaks*) decides to help rob them. What follows is a bizarre, horrible, funny fairy tale all set within the confines of the landlords' house, which contains far more than just hidden stashes of gold.

A parable about economics, its message – though blatantly clear – never threatens to get in the way of what it a terrifically entertaining movie.

THE LAST STARFIGHTER (1984)

The ultimate youth wish-fulfilment movie. Alex Rogan (Lance Guest) aces his scores on the Starfighter arcade game, only realising when he becomes the game's highest-scoring player that he's been auditioning for a real interstellar war.

A fun chunk of eighties sci-fi nonsense, enlivened by its cast and characters. It feels like, with a few more quid and a couple more drops of talent, it could have been a Spielberg movie but if that sounds like horribly faint praise don't be put off.

DEAD AND BURIED (1981)

From Dan O'Bannon and Ronald Shusett[7] we have this strange, terribly eerie and clever little movie about a small town where death isn't necessarily all it's cracked up to be. To discuss the plot too much would be to do it a disservice, but it has a touch of Stephen King to it and, while some of its twists and turns are signalled a mile off, it's all played out with such flair that it's hard to criticise.

---

7   Or possibly not; O'Bannon once claimed the script was entirely Shusett's and that he had nothing to do with it.

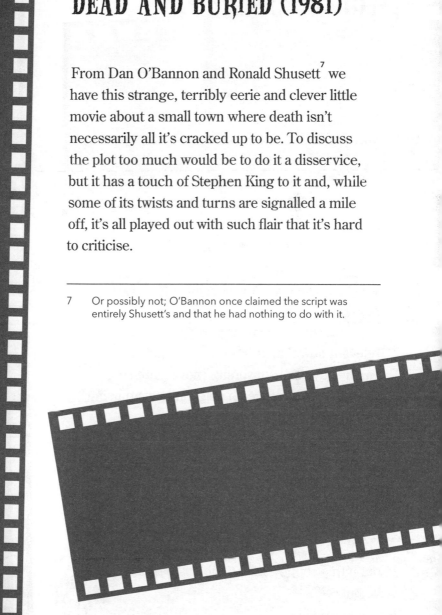

THE 'BURBS (1989)

I feel like I haven't talked about Joe Dante anywhere near enough in this book. *Gremlins, Innerspace, Explorers* ... he's a director whose work is littered all over the eighties (and beyond) and is never less than hugely entertaining.

The 'Burbs is a witty, dark comedy about the suspicion that breeds in suburbia. Tom Hanks leads a kooky selection of neighbours in an investigation of new arrivals, the Klopeks, who he believes are killing people. Naturally, their wives – including Carrie Fisher – are far more sensible.

A film whose theme is perhaps even more relevant now than it was then, it stands tall as an inventive and subversive movie with real teeth buried underneath its genuinely amusing, sometimes slapstick surface.

APENDIX 4

QUIZ ANSWERS

CHAPTER ONE

1. He throws a seven but needed thirteen. So the Demogorgon gets him. Obviously.

2. Sausage and pepperoni. Which is sausage and sausage frankly, but whatever.

3. The couch, that snuggly consumer of all lost things. I'm surprised they didn't look for Will there.

4. Midnight, Frogface, Toothless. Lucas considers Troy and his friend James 'assholes', and who are we to disagree?

5. His garden gnomes; like the rest of you I'm now terrified that, what with Will's disappearance, Hopper never got round to tracking them down. Hopefully, this vitally important plot point will be resolved in Season Two.

6. Coffee and contemplation. I agree.

7. An owl attacking Eleanor Gillespie's head because it thought her hair was a nest.

8. Kangaroos.

9. Miss Ratliffe.

10. Starch and cellulose. Though they are by no means the only polymers that occur naturally, there are many. Nancy could also have said rubber (which is often produced synthetically but is a natural substance), protein, chitin ... But she didn't. So no bonus points if you tried to show off. This is a quiz about the show, not a science test. I'm not Miss Ratliffe.

CHAPTER TWO

1. Penthurst, a 'nuthouse' that, according to Lucas is in Curly County. Perhaps he should be sent there because there's no such county in Indiana. But then, there's no Hawkins either so maybe they're all mentally ill.

2. Michael Myers, who, of course, came home in the Halloween movies.

3. 22 inches (which is, like, ten times bigger than Dustin's).

4. Their reclining chair. You get a bonus point if you correctly stated the brand: La-Z-Boy.

5. Camels.

6. Yoda it is.

7. Rory (though probably spelt Roary as he's named after the speaker in his mouth that allows him to do just that).

8. The answer to number eight is ... eight. I know, I'm such a tease.

9. 1923.

10 Summer of 1961.

CHAPTER THREE

1. AV Club.

2. Operation: Mirkwood. No, the colon isn't said out loud, obviously but code names always look better with a colon.

3. The war in Vietnam. (Yes, you were allowed to just say 'Nam.)

4. Space Lasers. Not such an outlandish idea given that President Ronald Reagan had just announced the Strategic Defense Initiative, nicknamed the Star Wars program. The SDI was a combined ground and orbital system designed to protect the US from nuclear missiles. It would have used laser weaponry to achieve this. Ultimately, it was decided that the initiative was too ambitious to be successfully realised.

5. Tom Cruise.

6. Nicole, and I suppose we shouldn't blame her, even though actress Glennellen Anderson delivers all the smug during the scene where Steve breaks Jonathan's camera.

7. Blow me.

8. Casserole.

9. The Tigers. The middle school team is called the Cubs.

10. He calls him a mouth-breather. Which is a common enough insult but a weird one. Presumably our IQ drops whenever we're suffering from a cold or get really out of breath.

CHAPTER FOUR

1. Gary, but he would have got bored cutting up a rubber facsimile so he was sent home.

2. Shepard.

3. "The brown current ran swiftly out of the heart of darkness, bearing us down towards the sea with twice the speed of our upward progress; and Kurtz's life was running swiftly, too, ebbing, ebbing out of his heart into the sea of inexorable time." A clue is hidden in the quote; the novella is *Heart of Darkness* by Joseph Conrad, the basis for the movie *Apocalypse Now* (1979).

4. Sandie Sloane.

5. Hideaway

6. ("It's a fancy word for") toothache.

7. The Satler Company, run by Frank Satler. He's a decent guy.

8. Patty

9. He forgot his hat. He's all about the lies in this episode isn't he?

10. Cujo. And he wasn't always, he used to be positively lovely until that pesky bat bit him.

CHAPTER FIVE

1. A toy lion and she's not the only one, Will also has one, as did Hopper's daughter. A clue for season two? Or, and without wanting to be Mr. Boring here I think this is more likely, did the prop department just hope we wouldn't notice? Bless them, they don't know sci-fi fans, we notice EVERYTHING, even things that aren't actually there!

2. Jennifer Hayes. She's played by Kaylee Glover, an eleven-year-old from Gastonia, North Carolina. Glover has worked as a model, and claimed she had no interest in being an actress but that her two days on set has changed her mind and she wants to pursue it in the future. When she auditioned she was told that crying on demand was a requirement for the role, apparently she imagined it was her mother in the casket. She cites her main inspiration as actress Dove Cameron.

3. Green, because he couldn't find the right crayon.

4. His ceiling light. Bet he wishes he'd checked there before ruining his sofa.

5. *Cosmos* by Carl Sagan. It was a TV series co-written (and presented) by Sagan, the book being published at the same time to complement it.

6. Hugh Everett, an American physicist and the first to propose such a theory. He was derided for it at the time and ended his physics career as a result. He's the father of Mark Oliver Everett (often known as 'E') frontman of the band Eels.

7. Dale and Henry.

8. *All the Right Moves*, the 1983 football drama featuring 'lover boy from *Risky Business*' and Lea Thompson, most famous for her waterfowl loving ways in *Howard the Duck* (and *Back to the Future* if you're going to be dull about it).

9. None whatsoever. Nancy, however, hits a can on her very first shot.

10. Nine, and, yes, Lonnie's King of the Arseholes.

CHAPTER SIX

1. The Indiana AV Club.

2. The boys couldn't agree on which direction to take so the trolls took them out one by one. I'm assuming this was a D & D campaign, either that or it's been a tad frisky in Hawkins, Indiana even before Dr Brenner started playing with alternate dimensions.

3. Robert. The store, Bradley's Big Buy, is a real one (though it now seems to be part of the absurdly-named Piggly Wiggly chain): it's in Palmetto, Georgia.

4. Four. I did the naughty clue in the question number thing. Sorry.

5. Bonsui.

6. Fourth grade.

7. During the third trimester.

8. Thirty percent. Bargain.

9. The Hawk.

10. Byers is a perv.

CHAPTER SEVEN

1. The corner of Elm and Cherry.

2. Russian.

3. $1.20

4. 3DS 46T2

5. Melted plastic and microwave bubblegum.

6. Fun. Dustin is not great at spur of the moment lies.

7. Bobbing for apples.

8. 1500 lbs, just over 680 kilos for the more metrically minded.

9. He rests an uncooked egg on the surface to see if it floats.

10. A fire extinguisher.

CHAPTER EIGHT

1. A Smiley. The Smiley as we know it - it is, after all a very simple image and similar designs are everywhere - was designed in 1963 by Harvey Ross Ball, a graphic artist who was paid forty-five dollars to come up with it. It took him ten minutes and it was originally used as a method of lifting the morale of employees at the State Mutual Assurance Company, Massachusetts.

2. *Anne of Green Gables*, written in 1908 by Canadian author Lucy Maud Montgomery (you didn't need to know the last bit, I'm just sneaking facts onto what would, otherwise, be a rather arid page).

3. I know, I know, that was horrendously easy but it's hard to find difficult questions for this episode, by question eight I'll be asking you what Eleven likes to eat, just see if I don't. The answer, as if you needed to check, is chocolate pudding.

4. Three or four minutes past ten.

5. "No more."

6. "Where am I?" Because he knows it's traditional.

7. A new mix-tape. You just know that going out with Jonathan would involve a LOT of mix-tapes.

8. See? I warned you. Now go away, I feel wretched.

9. Thessalhydra. He rolled a fourteen so I guess it won't try and kill him next series. Probably.

10. It's runny. So runny. I said there was no prize for this homework but, you know what? You got to see a grown man reduced to asking questions about potatoes. And his career.

NOTES

NOTES

NOTES

NOTES

NOTES

NOTES

RESOURCES

As well as the usual soup of scary Internet places where a writer dips his spoon in order to check dates and details (Wikipedia and the IMDb, neither of which are entirely trustworthy but let's be honest it's where we all start), sections of this book would be thinner were it not for the following:

Entertainment Weekly
    '*Stranger Things* premiere episode: The Duffer Brothers introduce their new Netflix series', 15 July 2016

Entertainment Weekly
    '*Stranger Things*' creators Duff Brothers: 7 facts to know', Nick Romano, 6 September 2016

Vulture.com
    '*Stranger Things*' Duffer Brothers on '80s Cinema, Fighting Over Kid Actors, and How They Cast Winona Ryder', Jen Chaney, 15 July 2016

Vulture.com
    '*Stranger Things*' Finn Wolfhard on Kissing Scenes and How He Became an Actor', Jen Chaney, 25 July 2016

North Carolina's *The News and Observer*
    'Durham's Duffer Brothers land on Netflix', Craig Lindsay, 9 July 2016

Rolling Stone
'*Stranger Things*: How Two Brothers Created Summer's Biggest TV Hit', Kory Grow, 3 August 2016

Rolling Stone
'*Stranger Things*: Meet the Band Behind Show's Creepy, Nostalgic Score' Christopher R. Weingarten, 1 August 2016

The Hollywood Reporter
'The Duffer Brothers Talk *Stranger Things* Influences, It Dreams and Netflix Phase 2' Daniel Fienberg, 1 August 2016

Bustle.com
'Winona Ryder's Casting In *Stranger Things* Wasn't An '80s Reference, But She Did Inspire One Of The Show's Best Nods' Leah Thomas, 23 Aug 2016

Backstage.com
'How Netflix's *Stranger Things* Cast Its Kid Actors' Benjamin Lindsay, 27 July 2016

DailyBeast.com
'Inside *Stranger Things*: The Duffer Bros. on How They Made the TV Hit of the Summer' Melissa Leon, 7 August 2016

Slash Film
Who Are the Duffer Brothers? Learn More About the Creators of *Stranger Things*, Peter Sciretta, 3 August 2016

io9
   '13 things you didn't know about Poltergeist' Meredith Woerner, 30 October 2013

Wired.com
   'The *Stranger Things* Secret? It's Basically an 8-Hour Spielberg Movie', 12 August 2016

What-song.com
   '*Stranger Things* Soundtrack (what a useful thing this was, though, fret not, I checked in case the Internet was lying)

Consequence of Sound
   'From Horror Legend to Rock Star: A Conversation with John Carpenter', Mike Vanderbilt, 17 May 2016

The Quietus
   'No Longer Lost: John Carpenter On Playing Live', Staff Writer, 15 February 2016

Billboard.com
   'John Carpenter Talks Debut Album "Lost Themes" & Why Music Is Easier Than Directing' Joe Lynch, 26 January2015

Vulture.com
   'The Soft-Spoken John Carpenter on How He Chooses Projects and His Box-Office Failures' Simon Abrams, 6 July 2011

Art of the Title, Richard Greenberg (and various other features that had nothing to do with the book but I got lost in this lovely, lovely site)

RogerEbert.com
  I Believe in Unicorns, Brian Tallerico, 29 May 2015

pressofatlanticcity.com,
  'Little Egg Harbor boy on road with national *Le Miz* tour'
Vincent Jackson, 24 March 2013

And look! Some actual physical books:

Easy Riders Raging Bull, Peter Biskind, Simon and Schuster, 1998

The Montauk Project: Experiments in Time, Preston B. Nichols and Peter Moon, Sky Books, 1992

The Art of Drew Struzan, Drew Struzan and David J. Schow, Titan Books, 2010